# BEARA WOMAN TALKING

*Peig Minihane, 1861–1957*

# BEARA WOMAN TALKING

## THE LORE OF PEIG MINIHANE

*Folklore from the Beara Peninsula, Co. Cork*

*Collected by*
Tadhg Ó Murchú

*Edited, arranged and translated by*
MARTIN VERLING

MERCIER PRESS

First published in English in 2003 by
Mercier Press
Douglas Village, Cork
Email: books@mercierpress.ie
Website: www.mercierpress.ie

Trade enquiries to CMD Distribution
55A Spruce Avenue
Stillorgan Industrial Park
Blackrock, County Dublin
Tel: (01) 294 2560; Fax: (01) 294 2564
E-mail: cmd@columba.ie

© Martin Verling 2003
ISBN 1 85635 417 2
10 9 8 7 6 5 4 3 2 1

First published in Irish in 1999 by
Cló Iar-Chonnachta, Indreabhán,
Conamara under the title
*Béarach Mná ag Caint: Seanchas Mháiréad
Ní Mhionacháin*
ISBN 1 902420 05 5

Cover design by mercier vision

A CIP record for this title is available
from the British Library

Printed in Ireland by ColourBooks,
Baldoyle Industrial Estate, Dublin 13

# CONTENTS

## ACKNOWLEDGEMENTS

I am grateful to the Head of the Department of Irish Folklore, Professor Séamas Ó Catháin for giving me permission to publish this material. I would also like to express special gratitude to Gearóid Ó Cruadhlaoich, Department of Irish History (Folklore), University College, Cork for all the help and encouragement he has given me since I began to work on the folklore of Beara.

More than any other individual, I am indebted to Noreen Heaney for the information she has given me about her grandmother, Peig Minihane. Without Noreen's contribution we would be totally dependent on the diaries of Tadhg Ó Murchú in order to get an insight into Peig Minihane's character and personality. As excellent as Tadhg's diaries are, there can be no substitute for the type of intimate knowledge provided by Noreen, who lived in the same house as her grandmother for so many years. Also, because she was present for some of Tadhg's visits, Noreen was able to provide a unique account of the actual collecting situations.

# INTRODUCTION

In 1895 Pádraig Ó Laoghaire, from the townland of Inches near Eyeries in the Beara Peninsula, Co. Cork, produced the first ever printed collection of stories in Irish from the oral tradition.[1] Since that time only one book on the folklore of that part of the country has been published,[2] even though there are around 7,000 pages of material from Beara in the manuscript collection of the Department of Irish Folklore, University College, Dublin. Without doubt the material collected by Tadhg Ó Murchú, a full-time collector with the Irish Folklore Commission, is among the most scrupulously collected of this 7,000 pages.

Tadhg Ó Murchú was born in the townland of Sceachánach near Castlecove in the Parish of Cahirdaniel on 11 February 1896. He worked as a full-time collector with the Irish Folklore Commission from 1935 to 1957. During this time Tadhg did an extraordinary amount of work, collecting some 60,000 pages of folklore. Tomás Ó hAilín wrote an account of this important work in an article in *Éigse*;[3] there are other shorter accounts of his work in *Béaloideas*.[4] But to get a fuller picture of Tadhg's background one would need to study the unpublished account which he himself wrote of his youth and native place.[5] Tadhg Ó Murchú died on 8 September 1961.

Tadhg did trojan work when he stayed in the village of Eyeries during the spring of 1939. In his search for suitable informants he travelled the rough and remote roads of the parishes of Kilcatherine and Allihies on his bicycle for three weeks, with the heavy Ediphone recording machine – or 'Eugene'[6] as he himself called it – on the carrier. The Ediphone weighed between three and four stone.

Having returned home to Waterville, Co. Kerry from Beara on 17 May 1939, Tadhg wrote to Seán Ó Súilleabháin, the archivist with the Irish Folklore Commission:

> I am like an old cart horse for the last few days after my journey around Cork – worn out and tired after my travels – and, indeed, it's no wonder! They were the hardest three weeks I ever spent, except for the fact that I got the weather I needed. I did a lot of travelling with 'Eugene' along bad roads – as bad as there are in Ireland

– but I am very happy with the results of my labours. I brought eleven dozen spools[7] with me and wasn't that a great amount![8]

It is important to remember that Tadhg had to transcribe the full contents of these recording spools when he went home to Kerry after his Beara journey. Anyone who has transcribed modern tapes will appreciate the difficulty of this work and the concentration required. How much more difficult it must have been to transcribe from these old wax spools.

Tadhg's task was all the more difficult because the Irish language and the tradition of storytelling – as it used to be practised at any rate – were in their death throes in Beara at that time. In spite of this, he succeeded in collecting about 1,000 pages of very valuable material during that spring of 1939. Tadhg payed other visits to Beara in 1950, 1951 and 1952 during which he collected a further 450 pages. In addition to this, there are 450 pages of his diary which describe in great detail all his experiences in Beara.

It was during the years 1950, 1951 and 1952 that Tadhg collected from Peig Minihane, of Gurteen, Ardgroom, the material on which this book is based, and without doubt it was a great achievement to collect this valuable lore from the 'mouth of the grave', from an old woman of ninety years of age. Were it not for Tadhg's diligence, and his understanding of the importance of the work, our knowledge of Irish folk belief and, especially in this case, of women's folklore would be much the poorer.

---

1 P. Ó Laoghaire, *Scéalaíocht na Mumhan* (Baile Átha Cliath: Pádraig Ó Briain, Clódóir, 1885).
2 P. Ó Murchú & M. Verling, *Gort Broc – Scéalta agus Seanchas Ó Bhéarra* (Baile Átha Cliath: Coiscéim, 1996).
3 *Éigse* 16 (1957), p. 113–30.
4 *Béaloideas* 28 (1960–62), p. 133; *Béaloideas* 25 (1957), pp. 150–52.
5 IFC 1252, pp. 3–572.
6 It was Muiris Ó Ríordán from Macha in Baisleacán, Co. Kerry who christened the Ediphone 'Eugene' (T. Ó Murchú, 'Scéalaithe do b'aithnid dom', *Béaloideas* 18 (1948), pp. 27–8).
7 The wax recording spools for the Ediphone.
8 The correspondence of Tadhg Ó Murchú, Dept of Irish Folklore, UCD.

# THE LORE OF PEIG MINIHANE

# LOCAL LORE

## LOCAL SETTLERS AND INHABITANTS

### *Coastguards in Ballycrovane*

There were coastguards west there in Ballycrovane as I remember. I remember four families of them there. They used to have young servant girls minding the children; the households (of coastguards) were of young men and women. Two of the families used to go to Mass, and the other two did not: I suppose they were English. Well, those who did not go to Mass used to wash the potatoes and do all the chores on Saturday. Those who went to Mass were not half as fussy as they were (about the Sabbath).

## MIDDLEMEN AND LANDLORDS

### *Máire Ní Ghearail' and Mac Finín Duibh*

Máire Ní Ghearail', I never saw her – she was gone years before I came to Ardgroom. She lived in Cuhig, the townland nearest to us here on the Kerry border, and she buried a canvas bag, I heard, that would hold five pounds of flour. She was making it for a week and nobody knew what she was doing.

Her husband was dead for a long time: she was a widow. She had a sister south in Adrigole and her son came looking for three pounds in money from her.

'Go out into the little shed behind the house,' she said, 'and get the spade that is there.'

He went out …

She brought the boy behind the house and took the spade with her.

'Do you see that place there?' she said. 'Scrape there with the spade, and when you come across the flagstone, take it up,' she said. 'It's in there.'

11

The boy did as she said. It was all gold – all gold is what she had – she had no paper but yellow gold.

She put her hand under the flag, when she raised the corner of the flag she put in her other hand and took out three sovereigns.

'Take that much,' she said, 'and maybe that's all I'll have out of it.'

The next day, she made the bag and she put all the gold into it, and when the night fell she was on the look-out in case any of the neighbours would see her. In the middle of the night she had the bag ready and she put her cloak around it so that nobody would see her and she travelled every road until she came to Mac Finín Duibh, and she gave him the bag.

'You nearly missed me,' he said. 'I am going away.' He recognised her. I suppose he had seen her before that.

'Dear Máire Ní Ghearail', how did you make the money?' (he said).

'I didn't steal it or rob it,' she said – which was the truth.

She gave him her bag of money and she never saw it again, because he was killed, the poor man – Mac Finín Duibh – and a collection had to be made later to put her in a coffin. That's what the old people of the district said – after she minding it so carefully, my dear!

She was always afraid that she would be robbed, you understand (and that's why she placed it under the care of Mac Finín Duibh – for safety).


THE FAMINE

1. *Graves by the ditchside during the Famine*
If I was to tell you where the graves of the people (who died during the Famine) were, you would not go outside the door (with the height of fear).[1] They are a little east of us, between us and the road east. They are there, dear (buried) … fell down with the hunger, and were buried where they fell.

2. *The picking of white periwinkles during the Famine (i)*
The people had nothing to eat but strand pickings, and they could find nothing (on the strand itself) but white periwinkles.

### 3. *The picking of white periwinkles during the Famine (ii)*
They used to be on the strand picking the white periwinkles; the black periwinkles were not to be found because they were picked and their seed gathered.

### 4. *Eating charlock[2] during the Famine*
They used to go pulling the charlock. They used to bring it home and cut it with a knife, finely, and they used to boil it and eat it.

### 5. *Watching the garden during the Famine (i)*
North in Claondoire, in Droinn a' Bhogaigh, they used have to, of their own accord, be watching the garden – one (at a time) always – during the Famine, in case their potatoes would be stolen from them. My own mother, when she was a little child, used to, she told me, spend many a night watching the garden.

### 6. *Watching the garden during the Famine (ii)*
The Famine came upon them before that when the people had to watch over the garden and the animals at night. They use to call them the Whiteboys – the people who stole during the Famine.

### 7. *Eating seaweed*
And another man who was working in a field, his wife came to him at dinnertime – she came to her husband who was working – setting [potatoes] I suppose – with a vessel full of seaweed gathered from the shore. And she boiled it and brought it to her husband for his dinner. When she came to her husband with the boiled seaweed he could not eat it, he threw it on the ridge.

### 8. *Working on the roads during the Famine*
Well, the year the road down there was made – The King's Road – there was not a house to be found but someone from it was working on the road for two fourpenny pieces a day, God love them! The Public Work Road is what it was called.

Well, my husband's father was working there as a young man, and someone complained him, that he could live at home (without the work) and he was sacked.

He stayed at home then and planted a little bit of a garden, and with God's grace, he said, they (the potatoes) grew there like the stones. God help us, those who did not stay at home and did not plant anything, they died of hunger.

## 9. Spike

When the road down there (the public road) from Castletown to Kenmare was made, eight pence a day was the pay, and many men were working there. That was the pay they had. But there was a man working there and a poor woman came to him on the road, with two children. And there was relief being brought out from Castletown to Ardgroom, and the man who was bringing out the relief, he had a horse, and he carried the bag of bread on the horse's back.

But when the poor woman came to them then, one of the men said to give her a bite of bread; that she was crying with weakness and hunger.

'Throw a piece of bread from the bag,' he said to the horseman, 'to the poor woman who is dying of hunger.'

'I certainly will not, wisha!' said he.

'Well, if you don't, you will give it whether you like it or not!' said the workman boldly

Right, he would not give it, and he (the other man) caught the bag and pulled it from him against his will, and he took a pound of bread from the bag and gave it to the poor woman. She then went inside the fence, and she sat down there and ate the pound of bread, herself and the two children, and she was dead by morning.

And the man [the horseman] from whom he took the bread brought him to law, and gave him a summons, and he was sent to Spike Island for seven years: that is what he got for taking the bread.

There was a boy then, the day he was left out, and he was the first boy to call him Spike – a boy from the island – and the man struck the boy. I suppose he gave him a good blow. But he struck him anyway. But he got another year for striking the boy.

From the day he was detained, and he was given that term (in prison), he never wrote a word to his wife, and there was no account of whether he was dead or alive. He came home, and she was about to marry a week later when he came home to her: he never wrote her a line while he was in Spike.

1 It was to her son's daughter that she said this – a bright cheerful girl, who gave me great help in reminding her of things. She told her to tell me about certain graves which were near the house – people who died during the Famine – who was buried in them and how they died, etc., and that was the answer she gave her – Tadhg Ó Murchú.
2 Praiseach bhuí.

# THE LIVELIHOOD OF THE PEOPLE

## 1. Gathering wreck on the Point

The Point [Kilcatherine Point] was a great place for wreck long ago, as many ships were sinking at that time. It's often that good men were drowned because of it, because wreck was only to be found where there were waves.

## 2. A boy who was drowned while after wreck

There was a woman there in Inward Ardgroom, Máire Houlihan was her name, and she had two daughters and a son. And he [the son] got up early one morning, and he went out unknownst to her, and she didn't know where he went until the news came to her that he was drowned. Whatever news came to her she threw herself out of the bed and, whatever name she called him [the son]: 'Is he drowned?' she said.

'He is,' said her daughter. 'He is on that strand to the north and there is deal [pine timber] beside him.'

There wasn't one rib of hair on her head but that she tore it out, and it never again grew before she went into the soil.

## 3. Bad luck that follows wreck

*Tadhg Ó Murchú*: Was there any belief here that no good luck followed wreck?

*Peig Minihane*: I used to hear about the [bad] luck all right; the person who never got a piece of it was just as well off as the person who got the greatest amount ever of it, because it was said that the person who went looking for wreck that he was looking for his death, as there was danger in the wreck.

Máire Ní Mhurchú[1] told my mother many things about wreck, and she would not allow any of her own family near it. Máire used to be warning them that there was danger in the wreck.

## 4. Live fish on Saint Patrick's Day

On Saint Patrick's Day, 'the live fish' was certain to be in any house that was near the sea … [shore] gathering no doubt. Well, they used to go, the men of the house, they used to go some time during the day to the shore and crack a few limpets. 'The Bacon of the Sea' the old people long ago used to call them (the limpets).

Well, when nobody would go to boil them and pick them out, the man of the house would go some time during the day and he would bring four limpets back with him – four of them – and he would throw one of them in each corner of the house – and up in the loft. He used to bring them home in his pocket, and it's often it was done here – in this house. 'Live fish on Saint Patrick's Day', I asked my own husband who was here, what the basis for it was. But he said to me that there was someone long ago who said that for anyone who would bring in live fish on Saint Patrick's Day, there would be fishing luck on that house for a year.

That was the answer I got from him anyway. I didn't ask him any more about it.

FISHING – GENERAL INFORMATION

### Catching crabs

There were crab's lairs on the strand where they used to get big crabs and, may God have a thousand pities on you, if it got a grip on anyone he would suffer!

That was the hard task, to take the crab from its lair. They used to bring a gaff with them, but some of them who didn't have a gaff used to bring a narrow stick with them and they used to stick it into the lair to see if it (the crab) would catch hold of the stick. And it's often that they did.

*Tadhg Ó Murchú*: Used the crabs be eaten here?
*Peig Minihane*: You may say that they used to eat them, with relish!

DROWNINGS AND SEA ADVENTURES

### 1. Two who were tragically drowned[2]

There were three boys there west, I suppose it is more than ten years ago now, in Cathair Caim. One of them was a carpenter, [Fenton] and he brought a boy with him, who came from America and had lots of money, and they brought a boat to Kerry (to Kilmakilloge) for timber. Fenton brought the boat with him and he brought the boy with him and they went east to Bunaw. The evening turned wild, and the publican in Bunaw told them to stay where they were until the next day; that the road (the sea journey) was very long before them and that the load was very awkward. And he followed him down to the pier trying to stop them, and the 'timber man' would not stop for him.

Right. The next day, they did not arrive, and everyone wondered what was delaying them. Some man who was up on the mountain saw a dark object out in the middle of the river, coming in towards Cathair Caim: the wind was from the north. He came down and told his story, and what was there but their boat, turned upside down, and there was no trace of the two men. They went down, three or four of them, to the strand – the strand was not far from them – and they pushed out a boat and went out, and the boat was there before them. The boat arrived but they were never seen again, dead or alive. Mike O' The Strand's son had £2,000 (this boy who came back from America and who was with Fenton).

They say that it is not right to be too bold at sea.

## 2. How a boat from Cróchán³ was lost

Oh, I remember that too – the boat that was coming from Cróchán. He had been in America and was in the boat coming from Cróchán. The boat went on a reef and he jumped into the sea and another boat took him on board – he was on top of the water. I suppose he could swim: if he couldn't he would have been as drowned as the rest. But the boat saved him anyway. But there was a woman who used to be going around (a witch I suppose) – it used to be said that she used to be in the company of those from the other world – but she said to his mother: 'There will be no day as long as she lives but that she will see his death bed (the sea). Every day that she would get up.'

He was drowned after that on his way from Sneem. The night was dark and they went onto some rock and they were drowned.

### 3. Micil of the Island[4]

Micheál O'Sullivan of the Island ... he lived in the Island – Inisfarnard – and a ship came into the mouth of the harbour from the west – west from the river – a foreign boat, and she was calling for a pilot. And he heard her, and he knew that she wanted a pilot. He called his son from the bed, and told him that the ship was calling for a pilot out in the mouth of the river, and he got up.

The father and son brought a small boat with them and they went out to the ship.

'What is troubling you,' said the man who went out, 'that you are calling for help?'

'I'm lost,' said the mate, 'and would you help us,' said the mate, 'to reach some harbour? If you do,' said he, 'you will get £5 into your fist.'

'What harbour do you want?' said O'Sullivan of the Island.

'Sneem,' they said. He went on board and went on the elm – on the tiller – and he brought her from the west into the river. When he turned up to go to Sneem, he turned too quickly: the point was under water and it caught the ship, and she stayed there ...

'Do you know what is going to happen to you here,' said the mate, 'if you don't do your job properly? Look at that block there with the axe in it. Your head is to be put on that block and your head is to be cut off you!

When he turned to the tiller to turn up to Sneem – it was the mate who put him on the tiller, you see – Micil ...

'Be very careful,' said the mate, 'and do your job properly.' When the ship hit the rock ... 'What's this?' said the mate.

'Rock to be sure,' said Micil.

'Do you know what you will do now?' said the mate to him. 'Throw off your clothes and jump into the sea, and if you can swim make your way to the land.'

The mate was a good man he said. It's often I heard him (Micil) talking about it. He threw off his clothes, and three others shaded him in case the 'butcher' who was going to cut his head off would see him. The man came to where the axe was and the block – the man who was going to cut his head off – and he asked them where he was.[5] They were looking for him and some of the sailors knew that he was gone – they did not want to have to look at him having his head cut off. And the ship was on her side on the cliff – she turned on her side. And they were looking for him, by the way, and the three of them knowing where he went – the mate and the other three. O'Sullivan was being searched for, and if he was, he wasn't found.

He made it to the land, swimming north, and told everyone his story, and he was put in hiding. And the pursuit was after him the next day – the army was searching for him – and I heard that an underground house was made for him – and he was going from place to place. The Kerry people sheltered him, and he used to do holidays for the Kerry people after that: they saved his life for him. There wasn't a grey hair on his head that night, and it was as white as snow in the morning: he had a white head as a result of the terror, God love him!

Oh, I remember him well no doubt (Micil). He had a house full of children in the Island. And there were three other houses there.

### 4. Drowned fishermen seen ashore

Well, there was a man coming from Castletown one day, and the evening was getting dark on him as he made his way west to Gortahig.

Anyway, he met five men – they came towards him from the west – and he had a donkey and cart, and whatever he had in the cart I don't know … and he came in to the side of the road when he saw the men coming towards him.

'Well,' he said, 'good evening to you, neighbours,' said he: he thought that they were his neighbours, and he didn't know where they were going until the next day.

Nobody answered him and he didn't speak to them (again).

The donkey stopped and stayed there looking after them.

*Tadhg Ó Murchú*: He didn't know them I suppose?

*Peig Minihane*: No, until he went home. When he went home the news was before him that their boat was lost the evening before that – the same evening. He would not believe that they were drowned because he met them on the road.

'We will go searching for them tomorrow,' said he. 'They made it to land somewhere,' said he, 'because they met me as living men in such and such a place on the road.'

They were searched for, no doubt, around every place where it was thought that they might have come ashore, and the boat was found wrecked somewhere.[6]


FISHING – FISHING BELIEFS

*1. Saying the rosary going into the seine boat*
When the seines used to go out together, there was a man in the boat and he used to make them say the Rosary going into the boat, or inside in the boat. He would be mad at anyone who would not be there in time, and he used to have his little bottle of holy water in his pocket.

*2. A prohibition against putting a drowned person's body into the boat*
They (the old people) used to say in their own conversation that it was not right to put the body (of a drowned person) into the boat. I heard that it was done here and that they caught no fish that year.

*3. A sheaf of straw to find a drowned person's body*
Tadhg Ó Murchú: Did you ever hear that the priest used to bless a sheaf of straw to locate the body of a drowned person?
Peig Minihane: The sheaf of straw? Of course I heard of it.

*4. Bartholomew's Day*
A boat sank out there in the mouth of the harbour on Bartholomew's Day …

'There is no roughness yet but a fart from Bartholomew,' the boatman said. The man on the tiller told them to pull for all they were worth, as it was getting rough …

*5. The mermaid and Paddy na mBó [Paddy of the Cows]*
Well, I didn't hear of anyone ever seeing her [the mermaid] except for one man who was always fishing: he wasn't beside the

sea at all but in a mountain glen. *Paddy na mBó* was his name. He saw the mermaid. He was fishing in Colleros, here to the north-east, with a rod, fishing away for himself. He came one day and he didn't catch anything, and he imagined that he might catch a strap of fish before going home because the day was fine. But he didn't. He went home and he came fishing again (the following day) to the same place: he didn't think anything you know, but he thought that the fish were not biting. Right. When he came the next day he threw out his bait and his line and he still wasn't catching anything. He looked around him and he saw a woman [mermaid] sitting on the cliff, below, where he was casting his line and bait and his lead.

'Oh Great Glorious God,' said he, 'I don't know who you are, or what is going on!' said he.

She came up to him.

'Why are you not catching fish?' said she.

'I don't know mistress,' said he – a little grey cloak around her, he said, and a grey cap on her head.

'Give me your hook until I see it,' said she 'your hook and your line.'

'Right. I will leave you now,' said she, 'and throw out your line and your hook and your lead,' said she, 'and I will leave you and you won't go home empty.'

In a minute there was no sight of her to be seen. When she was turning away from him …

'You are an honest poor man,' said she, 'and continue in your present ways always.'

Every day that came from then on that he wanted to go fishing – but he used not stay too long there – he would catch enough fish to keep him going for the year.

'We will follow *Paddy na mBó*,' the young people used to say, 'to see if we can see the mermaid.'

The neighbours who were in the glen where he lived – there are none of his people there now – used to say: 'We would have enough fish if we had *Paddy na mBó*.'

He never saw her again, but he used to go fishing and he used catch as much as he wanted to: it didn't matter what day of the year it was, he would catch the fish. It was in Doire Droinge, east of the mountain, east of Colleros school, that he lived (he was one of the Sheehan family).

FARMING – FARM AND DOMESTIC ANIMALS

*1. Calving – rubbing salt on the calf*
I saw the salt being rubbed onto the calf when it was born, so that the cow would lick it – rough or fine (salt). It is done.

*2. Putting a blessed candle under the cow*
*Tadhg Ó Murchú*: Used a blessed candle be lit under the cow when she calved?
*Peig Minihane*: I saw it done – the blessed candle. I did.

*3. The biestings being placed over the fire*
When the cow would be milked three times, it (the biestings) would be put over the fire in a bucket by the woman's hand. Before leaving the vessel out of her hand she used to make the Sign of the Cross three times over the fire with those first three milkings from the cow.

*4. The cows' hooves*
The cows that they used to slaughter for Christmas, they used to put the hooves over the smoke up in the chimney.

*5. Driving stock to the mountain*
I saw it in Kilcatherine. They used to put the cows – they used to have a few extra ones, strippers that would not take the bull at all – they used to put them on the mountain (in the summer) and they would milk them morning and evening, and bring the milk home with them.

*6. The goodness of the light brown cow*
A light brown cow – the goodness of the cow. They used to say that there was no goodness except in a light brown cow – 'The goodness of the light brown cow,' they used to say.

### 7. The first stripping

Well, I heard about that too (milking the first drop from the cow onto the ground), and the drop that came from the cow while the woman was milking her (that it should not be sought, because maybe it might be wanted by someone in the other world).

### 8. A prohibition against allowing milk out of the house

And they would not allow a drop of milk outside the door on May Eve or May Morning.

### 9. Making the Sign of the Cross over the cow

They used to make the Sign of the Cross over the cow's flank – the Sign of the Cross three times – on May Eve and May Morning.

### 10. Smearing with dung

Oh they used to, they used to smear the cows with dung (smear dung on their udders) on May Eve.

### 11. The cow that went dry and died

Oh, there was a man east there in Cuhig, one time, and the cows were settling down for the night near the house, and he heard a cow lowing after he went to bed, himself and his wife and family.

'I wonder what's wrong with the cow?' he said. 'I suppose I should have gone out and had a look at her before I went to bed.'

He thought that the cow was in season.

Right. He got up at dawn and the cow was there, and the cows – whatever number of cows were there. But he recognised the lowing of the cow: she was standing chewing the cud, he said. The next night – tomorrow night – he heard the cow lowing (again) – the same cow. She was lowing, and he heard her lowing going down from the house, from the cows' field.

He got up and put his head out the window – a little window that was there – and she was going down from the house. But upon my word, she was in the field before him in the morning, and if she was, she was sick and she had no milk. And he said that something was wrong …

'It doesn't matter,' his wife said. 'Maybe it would be better for us that she would go rather than one of the children – that she would go instead.'

But she was in eternity the following morning.

### 12. A hare milking a cow

Oh, there was a man here too, there west at the bridge (Ardgroom Bridge), and he was married up in Uxide, and he used to get up every morning: I heard him say it no doubt, God bless his soul. Well, he got up one morning then. He made out that it was a real hare – that it was how he had knowledge of it – and he fired at it too – a small stone – and if he did it went off and he was looking at it and watching it closely …

'I'm sorry now that I fired at you,' said he. 'Maybe you are not a proper hare,' he said.

He lost a cow within a fortnight after that. Oh, there are cows in eternity. There are.

### 13. The foal

Any foal that any eye (of a sinner) would not see being born, had curative properties, but if anyone was there while it was coming into the world, it had no cure in it.

### 14. The donkey man

There was a poor man coming from Castletown, and he had a donkey and cart, and the donkey gave up on him and he was giving the stick to the donkey – beating her with the stick.

And when he came east there just west of Ardgroom school, a voice spoke from inside a thicket …

'Don't kill the blessed animal, or if you do, you will pay for it.'

Oh, he didn't beat the donkey after that, he said, before he got home.

### 15. The speech of the animals

'It is raining,' said the horse.

'It is pouring,' said the cow.

'A beautiful fine day,' said the sheep.

'And jump the fence with me,' said the goat.

### 16. A prohibition against moving a cat from the old house

Tadhg Ó Murchú: Was it said that it was not right to move a cat from the old house when going to live in the new house?

*Peig Minihane*: It was not indeed (lucky to do it), but if it followed you in any way (of its own accord) there was nothing against it.

## 17. A prohibition against putting the dog after animals at night-time

They say that it is not right, if a dog was barking outside at night, and if it was a horse or anything that came from the mountain (around the house) that it would not be right for you to send the dog after it at night-time.

God's blessing on her soul, that woman I was speaking about (who lost her little girl), she had a dog, and he had the habit, from when the night would fall, of barking at a cliff that was outside the house – near the house. And it was night and she thinking of going asleep – there used to be horses coming from the mountain – and she felt something coming around the house. Right. She spurred the dog on east through the field from the house and she heard the person say: 'Don't set the dog' – in English.

Someone related to herself (from the other world) was doing it for her own good.

But upon my word, a couple of nights after that the dog died, God save us from the like of it! She was my brother's wife.

## 18. 'Hens a plenty and few cocks'

Oh, he was a rogue who used to be pretending that he had special knowledge, by the way. But there was this woman there and she had a hatching hen and she was going to leave her down – to put eggs under her. He met her and she told him that she was thinking of leaving down the hen and that she would like if all the chickens were hens …

'Place the eggs that you are putting down in a basin,' he said, 'and send for me and I'll come to you and I'll put the eggs under the hen.'

She sent for him and he came, and she gave him the basin and he put the eggs under the hen: two is what he took always (two at a time).

'Right, now,' said he to the hen woman, 'say, "hens a plenty", and I will say, "and few cocks". Right. I will put an extra one with them now,' he said. 'How many eggs do you put under the hen?' said he.

'Ten,' said she.

'Oh, put an extra one with them,' he said: 'that is eleven. If you ever leave down a hen,' he said, 'put an extra one with the eggs.'

But there was no good luck attached to them (to the clutch), only hens and cocks as she had always had them.

### 19. *The egg of the black chicken*
The first egg laid by the black chicken, it was good for the voice. A black chicken from the first clutch ... anyone who drank it cold, without boiling (it used to be said) that he would have a [singing] voice. 'Tis well I heard that – for three mornings, the first three eggs that she would lay, to drink them as they would come to you.

### 20. *'As dear as the two eggs for a penny'*
They used to be selling things from baskets on their backs – sweets and apples – and maybe there would be a house that there wouldn't be a penny in it, and they would give him an apple or a hank of thread or shoelaces for the eggs instead of the penny ...

'As dear as two eggs for a penny.'

### 21. *The March cock*
There was a woman long ago who used to wash the cock's legs first before she would put her own legs into it (into the water). There was a cock inside and they would not put him into any coop where the hens would be, but let him free around the house.

They used to say that it was good to have the cock in the house, and it's often I heard that: if any bad thing was going the road, if a March cock was in the house, that he would not allow anything inside the door. And there were some of them who used to keep a March cock: the cock that would be hatched out of the egg in the month of March – to keep him with the hens. And when a clutch would be left down that would have come from him, any house that would have that would be lucky – that no bad thing would happen in it. They would not give them the knife [kill them] ...

'You will kill him for Christmas' (a woman would say to another woman).

'Oh,' she used to say, 'I would not like to see the knife that would kill him. I would be thrown out!'

## 22. The cock's crow
If you heard a cock crowing at a certain time in the night that wouldn't be normal, they used to say that it was not good luck for someone in the house – anywhere that that would happen – if there was an old person there: 'The old man is to go: the cock is giving a warning' (would be said).


FARMING – TILLAGE, DIGGING AND SPADES

## 1. The setting of the potatoes
They did not like to do it – to set *sciolláns*[7] on Monday, and they did not like to plant on Saturday …

'Anything begun on Saturday, it will be a long time before it will be finished.'

They would not go digging the garden or setting *sciolláns* without starting on Saturday evening – to set a small bit. So they say: 'Don't break a custom and don't start a new custom.'

## 2. The blackening of the potatoes
The potatoes used to blacken … they used to blacken often long ago on them, and the boys used to say: 'The nails of my fingers is worn indeed, from peeling the skins of black praties.'

## 3. The Christmas ridge (i)
Oh, it was a custom here too – it was no doubt – a little bit of the garden that they used to harvest … they used to leave a bit of the ridge there for Christmas without harvesting it. I saw that.

## 4. The Christmas ridge (ii)
They used to leave – every last Christian of them – they used to leave a little piece of a ridge, the length of the rake there, for Christmas. And there was no Christmas Night but they would

put pieces of bog deal … they would have pieces of bog deal under the roof beam and they would put them under the potatoes [on the fire]. And when the potatoes would be boiled, they would take it [the bog deal] out of the fire and quench it with water, and it would be put under the roof beam again and it would be left there again for a year. It used to be called the Christmas Block. I don't know if it was to spare them [the potatoes] in case they would run short that they used to do it or not (to leave the little patch of potatoes without harvesting them.)

## 5. Beliefs concerning the spade (i)

It was the custom anyway that you should, when you stopped in the evening, if you did not want to bring the spade home with you, to throw it in the furrow.

And it was a custom with them too, when they would go to the garden or digging, when they would take up the spade – take the spade in their hands – that they would make the Sign of the Cross on themselves and on the spade, when starting work.

They used to bring in the spade and they used put it inside the door. And if they went out to a neighbour's house or anywhere (night walking), they would bring the spade with them, and put it on their shoulders then when they would be coming home – if it was late at night – for fear they would meet any spirit.

## 6. Beliefs concerning the spade (ii)

*Tadgh Ó Murchú*: The old people used to say that it was not right to put the spade on your shoulder inside the house. Was that a belief around this place?

*Peig Minihane*: Oh, upon my word, that is going on today as it was in those days – the axe or the spade or any weapon that would have iron in it, it is forbidden to put it on your shoulder inside the house. But any weapon that has steel in it – there is steel in the spade – if you walked Ireland with it on your shoulder you would not see anything [evil] or nothing would happen to you.

There was a man here some time ago, around this place, and he was digging for a relative, and he was late coming home at night, and he left the spade after him in the house where he was working. And, if he did, he saw something which frightened him and he became sick the day after: he was very sick. His mother went looking for Máire Ní Mhurchú and she told her her story.

'And did he see anything?' said Máire Ní Mhurchú. 'Ha ha!' said she, 'he didn't bring his spade with him. He left the thing that would save him from his enemy behind him. Well, I will do my best for him,' said she, 'but he will be sick for a while. I will do my best for him, but come to me again in a week.'

She was mad when he did not bring the spade with him – Máire Ní Mhurchú.

'He would have had what would save him on his shoulder,' she said.

### 7. Flax

Oh, upon my word, I planted it here myself a couple of years ago, and that is the flax that was troublesome.

*Tadhg Ó Murchú*: I suppose it was for sheets that you used to have it?

*Peig Minihane*: Sheets no doubt. Manure was put as fertiliser with it. They used to dig for the *sciolláns*, and they used to dig the ridges – to spread it [the manure] on the ridges then, and cover it like the garden.

They used to get the seed in Castletown, a pot or two – whatever amount would suit you. The children used to come then when that was covered and pick every little pebble, in case the seed would come up under them (and be smothered).

They used to beat it with the back of the shovel and they used to make it as level as the floor: after scattering it [the seed] they used to do the beating, and to pick the pebbles then. When they would have it shovelled, whatever clay would be in the furrows – when the seed would be scattered – they would put it on top of the ridge.


## BELIEFS ABOUT THE HOUSES OF THE PEOPLE

### 1. The closed door

*Tadhg Ó Murchú*: Wasn't there some old belief about the doors of the kitchen too – the door you would enter by, that you should not go out that door when you would be going … or the opposite, I don't know which?

*Peig Minihane*: They had that as a custom all right. I heard old people – an old man – saying that: 'Oh, from the west through the windy door [is bad] … nothing bad ever came from the east.'

The closed door or the windy door … it was forbidden to go out through that door. A woman who would be with child, she would only be allowed out the door that she came in through.

### 2. A glowing sod being carried around a new house

They would carry a glowing sod from the shed and they would go around with the sun, at sunset, on Saturday evening – around the new house – when moving from the old house to the new house.

### 3. Moving house on a Saturday

But they had another custom that they would not go into any new house on any day of the week except on Saturday evening.

### 4. Sleeping in the new house

And the first night they would sleep in the new house, another one of the neighbours – a girl, or a boy, or a man, or a woman of the neighbours outside – would sleep in the house that night with them. That is being followed still – a person not related to them to sleep in the house with them on the first night.

### 5. Coins under the corners of the house

I saw that no doubt, coins being put under the corners of the house. I was here when this house was built, and when the masons … the stones had been drawn by them, and when the masons began to build it, one of the masons asked me if I had any silver money. 'If you had a silver half-sixpence, or a sixpenny bit that they could put under the corner stones,' he said.

Well, the old man had two sixpenny bits that he used to have for tobacco: there were two silver sixpenny bits and a silver four-penny piece – they were on the go that time – he had them. And he didn't have the fourth coin at all, but he had two shillings, and I was sent west with the shilling and I got two sixpenny bits for it.

I was east of the house when I heard the whistle. He had a sixpenny bit and the old man asked him for it and he gave it to him, and they put them under the four corners – two sixpenny bits and a threepenny bit and a fourpenny piece – so that there would be money luck on the house.

I asked the old woman who was here what the basis for it was …

'Oh, so that there would be money luck on the house,' she said.

I never saw it in Kilcatherine (the custom of the money) anyway, I don't remember it.

### 6. A house on an old path

Oh, they would not build a house or an outhouse or a shed in any place where there was an old path. There was a man there west in Droinn a' Cheapaire, where the road turns north, west of the schoolhouse, there was a man of the *Reachtaire* family living in a little shanty, himself and his wife and family, that the door was so small on it that they could only barely get into it. He went to work and built a house there, in the level place – there was a rough place there too – and he built the house and left the little shanty.

Some man who was fairly old went … he went along the road by him …

'What are you doing there?' said he.

'I am building a house there,' said he.

'Don't,' said he. 'That is the corner of the old road that is going that way, and don't build any house there.'

'Ah nonsense!' said he. 'Those old roads are long since gone from the world.' He didn't do what he told him anyway. Right. He built the house there, and he left the place below – the shanty. There was no night, from when he started work there, that a light wasn't seen there from the King's Road – [by] the people who used to be passing by. Right. When the whole thing was going too far, this man (who gave him the advice) said: 'If he had only stayed where he was, but he was too bold, but let him follow his nose now!' said he – the old man.

He built the house, and the house wasn't a success for him, God save us from the like of it! And I don't know if the light is still seen there, but it's not long since it was. He became sick himself, and he wasn't long sick when he passed away and there were eight of a family after him.

## 7. Building onto a house
Oh, if you wanted to do anything with the house, to extend it – up from the house always [you should build].

## 8. A linny[8] on an old road
The man who was here with me long ago, he was going to put a little linny at the end of the house – a little linny that we would put the baskets and things into, you know. And this man came in here one day – a man who was great friends with us and good to us, anything we would ask him …

'Are you going to put a linny at the end of the house?' (said he to the man of the house).

'I am,' said he.

'Don't you know,' said he, 'that there is an old road going there, and don't put any linny there whatever you do,' said he.

So he built the linny back here, behind the house.

It is only a year ago – and I didn't tell anyone ever – since I heard the music and the noise going east here. It's there, the old road.

I heard the activity and the racket and the music and the talk – oh there was – going east. I asked the woman of the house east here if she heard any music going east over the house the night before that …

'I didn't,' said she.[9]

TRADES

## 1. Cutting rods ruring the November moon
They used to be watching the November moon to cut rods, and wasn't it great work that they couldn't make any basket with the rods that would be cut during any other moon. The rods would not work properly for them: they used to be cracking on them.

## 2. The blacking hole

There is a place down on the edge of the sea and there is a hole there that they call the Blacking Hole, and they used to take a lot of the stuff from the hole for dyeing.

## 3. Dyeing

There was never any good in any colour unless a penny was thrown into the (dye) pot first. The right colour would never come on the clothes only spotty grey, if you didn't put a penny or a halfpenny in the pot. And they wouldn't move the pot when the moon was coming up, and they wouldn't take the clothes that were being dyed outside the door until a day into or after the full moon.

## 4. The making of candles in Kilcatherine

I never saw my mother making candles, but I saw other people from home making them. They used to put the tallow [fat] melting – anyone who would kill a cow, and the person who didn't kill one would have no tallow – in a pot on the fire.

When they took it out – and they would dry it then outside under the sun – when it would be dry then, they used to put some of it in the pot and leave it boiling slowly. They would be taking it outside then, as it melted on the fire, to a jug: they used have big jugs.

They used to fill the jug with it then, and when it would be fairly cold, they would have a block about the width of that bucket there. And they used to have a tin candlestick (mould) and they used stand it in the block to keep it straight. They used to fill it with the tallow: maybe there would be three or four holes in the block, and the candlesticks standing there.

Then they used to put thread down through the candlestick, they used to have thread that they used to double, cotton thread, and they used to put a nail or something on the end of the thread and they used to put the thread down through the candlestick with a knitting needle, and they used to fill it with the melted grease then, and allow it to cool for an hour or two.

## 5. The making of old oil lamps

There was no oil being used at that time in any house for many years but that they used bring a shell by the side of the fire and some of this oil in it (the oil of horse-mackerel or the oil of small pollock) and a piece of rush. They used bring in a piece of rush and skin it – they would leave nothing on it but one little bit – that would be dipped in the oil then.

## 6. A little splinter hurdle

They used to break up the bog-deal with an axe, and the smooth pieces, without any knots on them, they would split for you without any bother with the knife, and they used to make a little hurdle from them. The small splinters were called *sceatacháns*.

## 7. Séamus of the ropes

*Peig Minihane*: And they used to make ropes from the bog-deal, and they used to know the piece that would make the rope after taking it up out of the [bog] hole.

*Tadhg Ó Murchú*: It wasn't every kind of bog-deal that would make the rope.

*Peig Minihane*: Oh, it wasn't. The deal that used be in the white clay, that would make a fire, but it wouldn't make a rope or *sceatacháns*: it was too brittle.

There was a man west here, and he was making his living on ropes (of deal): he didn't have a cow, a sheep or a horse, only himself and his wife and three daughters. He was known as *Séamus na dTéad* [Séamus of the Ropes]. The young boys used to be playing up on him, and what did they do but go in to him, one night, and they didn't say a word. And they caught the end of the rope, and there was a big coil of rope there after he spending the week before making it. Out the door with them, pulling the rope after them. He got up and caught the rope and they pulled him out onto the road, himself and the rope, a quarter mile of the road. How about that for trickery!

He used be selling the ropes and making a living on them, God love him, because he didn't have anything else. He had three girls: his wife was in eternity then: she was dead.

*Tadhg Ó Murchú*: What use did they mostly have for the bog-deal ropes?

*Peig Minihane*: On boats and a hundred things … on the haycocks – a haggard cock that would be made, saved, and using this rope, you would put two turns on the cock, and a good heavy stone, to protect the cock from the spring gales.

Well, when he would have a hundred fathoms, he would get a crown for every twenty fathoms, and there would be three strands in each of those ropes; twisted around one another, like the ropes that you see in the shops. The strands used not be stout at all – they used be narrow.

*Tadhg Ó Murchú*: How used he make the rope?

*Peig Minihane*: He used to make them on a form [bench]. There were three legs on the form – a fairly big form too. He used to put it [the rope] around the legs as he worked. He used to attach it to one of the legs at first, and around the others then.

He used have a fistful of these bog-deal shavings beside him – a shaving [ready] all the time – and be putting them in and twisting them: we used go to the door looking at him. Every Sunday he used to go gathering the bog-deal: he used not twist anything on Sunday: he didn't like to do it, indeed.

Well, he became sick when he got old, and there was a sister of his in the house with him when his family went from him. Yes, the priest was brought to him then, and the night he was anointed, he died that night, God's blessing on his soul and on the souls of all the dead, and on the souls of the dead of the world.

There were two men with her for company, two neighbours, and a woman (neighbour) – with the sister. And when they were about to take him down from the loft – there was a little ladder for going up to the loft – the pillow that was under his head was a pile of the rope, and what was folded inside the pile of rope – when they took it up in order to take him out of the bed to bring him down to the kitchen – but sixty-eight sovereigns – and he dead.

LUXURIES

*The making of snuff*

Oh, I did wisha, I saw the snuff being made no doubt, by an old woman, inside in a horn, a cow's horn or a bull's horn, or in something no doubt: the horn used be that length.

This old woman used to turn – she was here beside us – she used to turn a flag that was on the hearth and let it heat (by the fire).

She used put down the tobacco leaves on the flag – one by one on the flag. She used open the leaves then on her lap, and she used to rub them before she would put them in the horn. And she used have a little twig and she used to be pressing them into the horn.

She used put a cork on the horn then and put it aside.

1 A local wisewoman.

2 About twenty-five years ago. Fenton was from Reen in Caherdaniel parish, the boatman – the carpenter. I remember the night well – a rough squally night, with showers from the north. I was at home at that time – Tadhg Ó Murchú.

3 The Pattern of Cróchán (29 July, Pattern Night), at Comhad Graveyard in Bord Eoghain Fhinn. A full boatload from Beara side was drowned, God protect us, going across Kenmare River – returning from the Pattern. They were caught in a bad shower and a squall and the boat was overturned – Tadhg Ó Murchú.

4 This adventure of Micil of the Island was an epic of the seiners on the Kerry side of the River. The boys from the Beara side and from Bord Eoghain Fhinn, when they used to meet over in America, they used to describe it in the form of a conversation: 'Rock,' says the captain. 'Rock to be sure, sir,' said Micheál. She was a new ship in her first season. She belonged to the captain himself, and he was crying profusely down from his two eyes when she was broken, I used to hear my father saying – Tadhg Ó Murchú.

5 It seems that that was the law of the sea during those times ... the person who would take responsibility for the ship on himself – to pilot her – if he did not do his job properly, his head was to be forfeited instead of the ship if anything happened to her – Tadhg Ó Murchú.

6 The five men were [already] drowned when he met them – Tadhg Ó Murchú.

7 Small or split potatoes used as seed.

8 A lean-to

9 She didn't go any further with the story then: she didn't let on to the woman east that she heard anything – Tadhg Ó Murchú.

# THE COMMUNITY

*1. Schooldays in Kilcatherine*
The place where I went to school was out in Ballycrovane at the Coastguard Station. The school I was in was thatched; there was no slate on it; there wasn't, dear. But a new school was built in Kilcatherine then.

While I was at school I didn't speak a word of Irish. It was a master we had at first, and when the new school was built then (in Kilcatherine) he was sent west to Urhan. Stephen McCarthy was the first master we had. He was from Canfie.

I suppose I was ten years before I ever went to school.

We used to be learning the English at home – the boys who came before me, they used to be learning English.

Oh, there were many of them coming, no doubt, who had no word of English except broken English. When some of them came – poor girls who had nobody to teach them – they used only have broken English. But the mistress used to be questioning them …

'Tell me now,' said the mistress – the mistress was an outsider, who was in Eyeries, and she used to walk every day from Eyeries to Kilcatherine and a little dog with her – Tiny. She had no Irish no doubt. Right. She asked the little one the first day she came to school: 'Where does the man wear his hat? Is it on his leg or his hand?'

'On him head,' said she.

But this master from Canfie who was in Ballycrovane, from the day I went to school until the day he left, no day came but that he used to give me a half-pint bottle when they used to be out at play (the other scholars) – every day, regularly – to go to Eyeries for a half-pint of whiskey, and I would be (back) from

Eyeries before the scholars came in from play. Oh, upon my word, whether I knew my lesson or not, I wouldn't get any slap (from him). Two pennies was what he used to give me every day for going for the whiskey.

Between nine and ten o'clock we used come to school. Master O'Dwyer who came to Kilcatherine school after that, there is no morning in the year, [even] if it was snowing heavily, but that he used go swimming in a little cove which was beside Ballycrovane, on his way to school from Eyeries.

*Tadhg Ó Murchú*: Walking he used be, I suppose?

*Peig Minihane*: Walking no doubt, and the mistress too. Every morning of the year he used go swimming in this strand – Trá Chéim[e]. He used go swimming every morning in the year.

*Tadhg Ó Murchú*: What used ye be doing in the evening after school?

*Peig Minihane*: We would get a piece of bread and a basin of oatmeal [porridge] after coming from school, in the summer. We would go to the mountain then minding the lambs and putting them into a little hut made of stones, in the mountain – they would be put in there from the fox. It was in Leaca na nGearrcach that the little hut was. There was a big long wide flagstone, and they made a little wall under that to keep the sheep in, and a door on it. The sheep of three or four houses used be in it.

## 2. An old school and schoolmaster in Ardgroom

There was an old schoolmaster west there in Ardgroom, and he was there for a long time, and where he had the school was behind the church which is there now. And when he used be walking alone he used be talking to himself – he was living in Canfie. But he used be talking to himself going along the road – you would think that it was a revenue[1] [crowd] that was coming.

The old man who was here was going west one day looking for tobacco, and he [the master] was coming east against him and he talking to himself: 'Ho, ho, ho!' he used to say, 'a French penny I got.'

He used to have a bad penny and he wouldn't get any tobacco for the penny. That was his way always when he left the house, to be talking to himself.

But the church was small. They built onto it. They made it bigger and that was the end of the school then.

*The post*
They would have to go west to Eyeries: there was no post nearer than Eyeries, and when the clerk used come (to Ardgroom – the priest's clerk) every Sunday, he used to enquire in the post office if there were any letters for the Ardgroom people, and he would let them know then. You would have to go west to Eyeries then for your letter – you would no doubt.

RELIGIOUS MATTERS, CHURCHES, GRAVEYARDS, PRIESTS & STATIONS

*1. Improper baptism*
There was a girl east there in Colleros, and she herself and (another) girl who used to be with her every Sunday going to Mass, and they didn't go to Mass at all this Sunday – maybe the Sunday was bad. This Sunday evening that this happened, she went cutting a 'bribe' for the cows – ryegrass. But the girl was with her, who used always be with her, and the two of them were going off together and they went into a ruin which was before them on their way, playing. Who was inside in the ruin before her but her grandmother who was dead for a year before that, and she recognised her. When she was going out, the other girl went out before her, and when the other girl was gone she [the grandmother] spoke to her: 'Be off with you now,' she said, 'and when you go home, throw the holy water on yourself, and don't throw it on the other girl at all.'

She fell sick by evening, badly, and she was pretty sick, and the priest was called. When the priest came she was bad, and the mother told the priest what happened to her.

'Ah,' said the priest, 'it wasn't I who baptised her, and if I did she wouldn't see any fairy.'

'And who baptised her, Father?' said the mother.

'A cracked little priest who was in the parish, but if it was I who baptised her, she wouldn't see any fairy.'

Well, the eldest of my family, who was in this house, the day she was baptised, it was an old man – a relative of the child's father – who was put standing for her, and a girl from Kilcatherine who was related to myself.

'Is it you,' said the priest, 'who is to stand for this child?' – when he moved into the place where she was to be baptised.

'It is Father,' said he (the old man).

'Do you know your prayers?' said he.

'If I didn't Father,' said he, 'I wouldn't be standing for a child.'

'Maybe you would need to be as good as you are,' said he (the priest), 'and if you don't know your prayers, don't stand for the child.'

### 2. Going for confirmation

The man who was here with me, [it was on] the same day his father and mother were confirmed, and they were eighteen years of age [the parents], and the church was full of old people going for confirmation the same day.

### 3. Kilcatherine church (i) the iron cat

Kilcatherine, there is a picture of a cat over the door lintel – it is there very obviously too – and any strangers that came there, it was looking at the iron cat they used to be.

Well, old people who were (living in the place) said then that those walls were built in one night and every little bit of those walls, there is nothing in them but stones from the strand: they gave some time on the strand before they came there.

### 4. Kilcatherine church (ii) a bull that died

Well, I had a couple of words to say about Kilcatherine graveyard.

There was a man in Kilcatherine, not too far from the graveyard. And Con Crowley had a bull … he was living beside the graveyard. The man came with a cow to the bull one evening, and the bull was so bad that he – Crowley – used have to stand in the field while the cows were being milked. The bull was cross, and anyone who came to the bull, they used only let the cow into the field and run off themselves – leave the cow there to him, in case the bull would come after them.

Right. This man came with a cow, and he drove her into the field and he went into the graveyard himself, and the bull didn't look at the cow at all, only followed the man. I remember it (to happen). I guarantee you that the bull knew where he had gone, and it followed him, and when he saw the bull coming, up with him into the ruin. And there was a window at the back of the ruin, it is there now and will always be there – a long window, narrow, and it is fairly high. In with the man, and in with the bull after him: the man imagined he would be all right if only he could get in through the window. He was barefoot in his shoes: he had no socks only the shoes. Up with him … he went into the window, and up with the bull and it put its snout up to see if it could come at him. And it brought the shoes with it: it tore them from his feet with its mouth, and the poor man keeping a grip with his hands on the stones of the window. Right. He was calling and calling for someone to come to his aid to free him: there was nobody around but the Man Above – calling on Him to help him.

Right. He was trapped, God love him, and the bull coming, trying to eat the feet off him. He made up his mind then, that he would try something else to see if he could get any help.

It wasn't long until he heard the belting and noise and the racket, and he said to himself that he had no chance but to jump back into the ruin to save his soul and his body. It wasn't long until he heard the belting and noise again, and the beating of sticks, and he saw nobody. Soon he saw the bull running back from the ruin, a little while after the beating and the belting and the racket. When he saw the bull going a little bit back from the ruin, he jumped down inside the ruin …

'Thanks be to God,' he said, 'that you didn't cut the feet off me!' he said, and he went out the northern door and went east out of the graveyard. Right. He survived anyway, and the next morning when someone was going along the road they saw the bull dead at the door of the ruin.

He was trying then – the brother who was living at home

beside him – to persuade him to go with him so that he could burn it (the bull); so that he would have that much satisfaction out of it. But the brother wouldn't go with him.

*5. Kilcatherine church (iii) how a warship scattered the northern side of it*
A big ship, the likes of which never came before, came into Kil-catherine Harbour, and stayed for a week there – the big ship.

She was out west in the mouth of the River, bellowing, call-ing for a pilot to bring her east to the harbour as the ground (the sea) was not too calm: it was rough enough. A pilot came to her too who brought her east to the harbour, and he got £5 – Tadhg O'Leary who was in Gurteen² – *Tadhg a' Dána*.

She gave a week in the harbour then; this big ship. Since the beginning of time no ship as big as her ever came into the har-bour.
*Tadhg Ó Murchú*: Do you remember her?
*Peig Minihane*: I remember her well. Well, this ship spent a week in the harbour when she sent a message back to him to bring her west again because the sound was very narrow. But he had good experience of it *(Tadhg a' Dána)*. He wasn't living far from the place where the ship was either: it was by the sea, his house. The day before he left then, the captain told him to come on board the next day at ten o'clock – *Tadhg a' Dána*. He went on board to him, and he was on board when he (the captain) did what I am about to say. When he was west out of the harbour, *Tadhg a' Dána* was on board her, so that he could bring her out of the storm which was [blowing] hither and thither …

'What kind of ruin is that over there?' the captain said to *Tadhg a' Dána*.

'A graveyard,' said he, 'where the people are buried.'

What did he do but to turn the big gun on the graveyard, and he put the northern side ... he scattered the side out of it, most of it, with the gun. I suppose he had no humanity, whatever kind he was (the captain).

He died on board before he got to any other harbour: I sup-pose he had no conscience, but that was true.

Oh, it's many a person who said, 'The death of the cats to him!' when the story came on board: *Tadhg a' Dána* was on board when he fell (dead). *Tadhg a' Dána* had a small boat, you know, to bring him ashore. But I guarantee you that it wasn't thinking of death or the other world that *Tadhg a' Dána* was: he thought that they would throw him out into the sea. The northern side (of the ruin) is open still: nobody put any hand to it (since).

## 6. *Kilcatherine church (iv) the priest's grave*
*Tadhg Ó Murchú*: Used there be any journey [pilgrimage] made to any place in Kilcatherine?
*Peig Minihane*: There used to, to a priest's grave in the graveyard, inside the ruin, in the corner of the ruin, just where you would go in the door. There are two doors (now) on it, but there was only one door on it in the beginning – the door was on the south.

## 7. *Clochán a' tSagairt [the Priest's Cairn] (i)*
There is one of them, a cairn, south of the mountain here, directly south, and that is the name of one of them, *Clochán a' tSagairt*. There is a big pile of stones there, where they used to say Mass. There is a nice field there, about twice the width of this house, where these cairns are in the centre of it.

## 8. *Clochán a' tSagairt [the Priest's Cairn] (ii) – priest hunting*
There was a priest west in Ballycrovane, in The Wood, for a long time. He used to be running from the Jews (the English).

There is a cairn up in the mountain there where he used to be saying Mass. *Clochán a' tSagairt* they call it. Well, he was there when the man who was married to me was born. They went west to The Wood (with him to baptise him) and he was two months old when he was baptised. They went from there to Eyeries from Barra Coille up there: it's there they were living. They didn't know where the priest was but to go and look for him (take a chance that he would be there before them). He was gone ahide maybe in some place. Well, they came home and went the next day and they went across the mountain to Castletown and the child with them. Right. They got a priest in Castletown anyway. He baptised the child for them, and they came home. I don't know … there was some strength in them (the old people), with the grace of God. Oh, may God not blame us for complaining now, dear, there is a good life in it compared to that time.

The 'Priest of The Wood' they used to call that priest who was west there in Ballycrovane, but I'm not sure what other name he had.

## 9. Station[3] bread (i)

The priests who used to come for the station to the people at that time, when they sat inside for their breakfast they would ask the woman of the house if she had any cake baked that had any meal in it. Well, if she had it then she would say that she had, and they would ask her to show it to them. She would be ashamed to show it to them … there would be too much meal in it (people would be ashamed long ago if they were using yellow meal bread or 'mixed' bread).

There was a priest at a station in that house up there – in Roger O'Sullivan's house that is there now – in Barra Coille. It was to his mother (that this happened) … and there was a priest at a station there. They used to be out on the mountains before that, on the run (the priests). When she put the breakfast before him (she said): 'I don't like the breakfast I have for you, I don't like it,' she said, 'but I didn't get the things I wanted.'

She didn't like the spoons she had, and she left aside a couple of them.

'Well, ah don't be any bit ashamed about it,' he said. 'It's often, and I minding the sheep, that I ate the eggs with a little twig of heather!'

## 10. Station bread (ii)

There was a priest here who was born and reared in Kerry, and there were a good few of them – every last one of them nearly – and when they would be for breakfast at the station – the priests – they used to ask, when the white bread was being put on the table, if they had any meal and flour bread. But I was at a station myself and the priest asked the women of the house if she had any meal and flour bread. She said she had but that it was for the use of the house.

'Give me a piece of it on the table,' he said.

'Oh I wouldn't like to give it to you, Father,' she said, 'because there is too much meal through it.'

'Bring it here to me,' he said.

She brought it to him – a small little cake of it. He took it between his two hands.

'Do you say,' said he, 'that this is yellow meal bread?'

'I do call it that, Father,' said she.

'Ah,' said he, 'you saw no hunger! Do you boil the yellow meal in the pot on the fire, and do you make porridge from it?' said he. 'If you were over in Kerry,' he said, 'where the Nashes are, it's many a pot of porridge you would have made in the last month, never mind the rest of the year. If you don't give yellow meal,' he said, 'and make bread from it, to your family, they will turn out delicate.' The *cáidí* was called *arán cabhra* here.

---

1 The informant used the English word 'revenue' which in Irish conversation could mean a crowd of people, flock of hens etc., depending on the context.

2 The townland of Gurteen referred to here is near Eyeries village and should be distinguished from the Gurteen east of Ardgroom village where Peig Minihane spent her married life.

3 This refers to the 'station' Mass which took place in the houses of the people. This custom continues to the present day.

# HUMAN LIFE

## 1. The birth mark

Did you see a mark on a person who had come into this world?
There was an old man here who had it on him, God's blessing on
his soul – a birth mark.

But they said that there was a cure in the hand of a person
who would be laid out dead; that a such a person would have a
cure when he would be laid out at his wake; that it (the dead person's hand) should be rubbed on the birth mark – and the Sign of
the Cross made over the mark nine times, three mornings – that
it would remove the birth mark to make the Sign of the Cross on
the birth mark. For every person who used to do it there would be
two who would not do it, because they would be afraid.

## 2. A caul on a child's head

*Tadhg Ó Murchú*: I suppose you heard of children having a caul on
their heads coming into the world?
*Peig Minihane*: They used to indeed, and I saw it no doubt; and
the person that I saw it (on), he is over in America.

I never saw it only on one person, and I'll tell you what the
woman who took it off him did.

When the child was born she saw it anyway. I was there too
but I didn't notice it. She was a neighbour woman. She took it off
the child: there was no midwife there only her. She told what he
had on him.

She took it and she put it on a strainer and she put the strainer over the fire to dry it, and she said that no living person on
earth should come near it: it was spread out on the strainer.

She took it in her hand and spread it out – it was like a little
piece of cloth – and she put it up over the fire.

The next morning she took it and brought it down into the room to the child's mother:

'When you get that dry,' she said, 'put it into the pillow under your head, and don't ever take the down out of the pillow.'

'Why?' said the woman.

'It doesn't matter to you,' said she.

She didn't give her any information.


## The Wedding and Married Life

### 1. A married couple racing one another out of the church

There was a couple here in Eyeries who married – and the priest had a laugh the same day – and the young girl got a warning (from her people) at home not to allow the young man to be first out of the church. But when they were leaving the church, they got tangled up – stuck together – trying to get out the door, trying to see which of them would be first out.

### 2. A prohibition against mothers

I heard it indeed – that it was not right for the mother to go to her daughter's or her son's wedding, or to go to the funeral of the first child.

### 3. The strawboys

Oh they, the strawboys used to be there too, and I tell you that they were the sport at weddings; and the straw that used to be on them was wheaten straw, because it was strong – and ribbons flying in the wind. And they used have a cap made up out of the straw. Anywhere there were children they used become terrified when they saw them; they used have to be put ahide. I don't remember them to have any music, and they wouldn't come in for a good while.

*Tadhg Ó Murchú*: Used they [the people of the house] be trying to tear the straw off them in order to recognise them?

*Peig Minihane*: *Erú*, the women and the girls, they used to tear it off them.

Oh, they used to dance too. Oh their captain used be out in front of them, dearest friend. They used have a captain too.

## 4. The stepfather who got rid of the child

Well, there was a farmer somewhere long ago, and it's often I heard it and it would be hard for me not to have it (the story), but when it goes with the wind it goes with the wind!

Right. He was married, and they had one child – a boy – when the farmer died, and a while after his death the wife got married again to another farmer from the area. The child was a year old then and he (the stepfather) said to the woman that he would take him out for a walk in the fresh air. He took him out on his breast like this to a place where there was a river and a lake beside it – part of the river was a lake. What did he do then only – I suppose he thought of drowning the child in case he would become an heir – yes, he threw him into the water, the child: he had him in front of him on a horse in order to get rid of him. And he got rid of him too …

'You'll pay for it,' said the voice speaking above him. He looked around him and saw nobody but he heard the voice.

'Who will pay?' said the man.

'Oh,' said the voice, 'your son's son after him.'

'Oh,' said he, 'if it goes that far, let him!'

But he came back and his wife asked him where the child was …

'Where is the child?' said she.

'*Erú*, I don't know where the child went,' he said. 'He was swept from the front of the horse from me,' said he, 'and I don't know where he went.'

'Oh you rascal,' said she. 'I'll send the guards after you,' said she. 'It's how you got rid of my child!' said she.

*Tadhg Ó Murchú*: But was he arrested then?

*Peig Minihane*: Oh, he was: the guards arrested him and he was put in prison, and when he was going to his death – he didn't live long in prison: I suppose he didn't like it …

'Where is the child?' he used to say and he on his death bed. The child was troubling him.

## SICKNESS

### 1. A bone that came out of a man
There was a woman up there in Cuhig, at the foot of the mountain, and I heard that she had a bone in her pocket until she went into the ground – a bone that came out of some sore that was on her husband.

### 2. A disease of the leg
And she had two daughters in the house with her (Mrs Mehigan),[1] and one of them married a boy who came from America or somewhere – they had a public house.

He was married to her a year. She was fairly old: they had no children. But this boy was there, a lovely friendly boy, strong and healthy, and one night like this, and he in the bed, he felt something niggling at his big toe. But in the morning when he got up he said that he didn't sleep a wink that night with the blinding pain in his big toe. Yes, it was niggling at him all the time, and that's the big toe that caused his death. He went to Dublin [to hospital] then but nothing could be done for him.

## DEATH

### 1. 'A respite until death'
'A respite until death' and 'a respite before death'. They had these sayings too.

### 2. Provision for death
And they used to say, you know, if the sick person ate anything extra (before he died): 'Oh, provision for death,' they used to say. That was said no doubt.

### 3. The making of the coffin
*Tadhg Ó Murchú*: Who used make the coffin for the dead person?
*Peig Minihane*: Anyone dying here, for years, it's a carpenter who makes it, but in olden times they used to bring a handyman with them to make it – buy the timber themselves. They used not take any pay (for making the coffin).

## 4. Opening the windows to leave out the soul

The windows and doors used be opened (when the soul would be leaving the body).

There was a woman west in Kilcatherine, and she was, as you said, drawing her [last] breath. She had two sons. One of them was married in another house and the other was married in the house where she was. Her eldest son was beside her holding the blessed candle in his hand in the candlestick, and he said: 'Let ye open the door – she is drawing her [last] breath – and leave out the soul.'

'Oh,' said her son's wife, 'let the soul go up the chimney if the smoke doesn't choke it!'

All belonging to the old woman were mad at her for saying that, and she was a strong woman (at that time), and there was only a year between her and the old woman when she died herself.

## 5. Protecting the soul from the hounds

Here, when a person would be dying, any morsel of bread or anything that the sick person would be using (they used to say) should be thrown out when the person was dying – thrown out to the hounds that would be watching the soul, to entice them away from the soul.

## 6. The habit

It wasn't put on anyone ever except somebody who would be in the Order. But even so these women who had knowledge said that the Order was no help to you unless you said the proper prayers morning and evening.

## 7. A prohibition against down

And none of them would allow any pillow that would have down in it … it wouldn't be put under the head of the corpse in the coffin, only hay: they had something against putting goose down under their heads.

## 8. Laying out the corpse

Tadhg Ó Murchú: Where used the corpse be laid out here?

*Peig Minihane*: On the rack – the seat – their faces south and their backs [feet] north. Wherever the seat would be before that, it would have to be arranged like that.

### 9. The candles of the dead (i)
*Tadhg Ó Murchú*: Was it a custom here to light twelve candles and to be going around the bed with them while the person was dying?

*Peig Minihane*: Well, if you were short any candle would do. But anyone who wouldn't have any candle for the dead (a blessed candle), they used say that twelve candles should be lighting while the soul was leaving the body. I saw that being done too, by a man: going around with the candle in his hand. (That would be done) if the bed was away from the wall (room between the bed and the wall).

### 10. The candles of the dead (ii)
*Tadhg Ó Murchú*: How many candles used be lighting on the coffin?

*Peig Minihane*: Five candles for the person who was in the Order, but four would do the person who wasn't.

### 11. The wake pipes
They used to bring them with them in a handbasket (pipes left over after the wake) and they used to leave them on the grave. Anyone who wanted to take one of them then, there was nothing to stop him from taking it.

### 12. Keening the dead
The old people long ago, when they died, laments used to be composed for them. But there was a man and he was dead: he was a young man too, but he was married and something happened to him. Right. His sister was beside him, and he was laid out and the sister was crying and crying.

But the sister said ... the wife was sitting at the other side of the house and she wasn't saying a word: 'Oh woman beyond,' said the sister, 'of the silken hanky, won't you come over,' said she, 'and lament your husband.'

'Oh,' said she, 'a man I will get, if I'm not old, and a brother you will never get. And lament him!'

### 13. Leaving a person in charge of house and corpse
Oh, the corpse should not be left on its own, no doubt, and a person should stay in charge of the house (when the funeral would be gone).

### 14. Leaving things in the coffin
*Tadhg Ó Murchú*: Did you ever hear of anything being put in the coffin with the body – the old man's pipe or his stick or anything like that?
*Peig Minihane*: Oh it's no harm to put a certain thing belonging to you (a special sign) in the coffin.

I have a little hammer there and I'm very careful about it, so that it will be put in the coffin with me when I die.[2]

### 15. A prohibition against crying
*Tadhg Ó Murchú*: Was it prohibited here to do any crying over the corpse for a certain length of time after a person's death?
*Peig Minihane*: If there was any old person inside, and if there was any relative of the person that died there (who wanted to cry), the crying would be stopped for an hour. Wisha, I saw that done no doubt.

### 16. Taking the corpse out of the house
The clothes would be thrown out on the floor when the corpse was being taken out of the bed. And the chairs from under the coffin … as it was being taken out the door, they would be laid upside down on the ground when the coffin was taken off them.

The legs would go out first (the corpse used to be taken out through the door with the legs forward).

### 17. A prohibition against bringing a corpse into the house
*Tadhg Ó Murchú*: Was it a belief of the people long ago, that a drowned person's corpse would not be allowed into the house, to wake it?
*Peig Minihane*: They used not do that either, or anybody who died

outside, with the grace of God, used not be taken into the house at all, but used be laid out in an outhouse, outside.

## 18. Bearna na Marbh [the Gap of the Dead] and Pointe na Marbh [the Point of the Dead]
It's east there, east of the school (Colleros School) where the arch is (going under the road), *Bearna na Marbh* [the Gap of the Dead], and *Pointe na Marbh* [the Point of the Dead] is east down from it (by the sea).

Funerals going to Kilmakilloge, they used to turn down there.

## 19. A prayer said going into the graveyard
I was one day at a funeral going into a graveyard north in Bunaw (Kilmackiloge Graveyard), and there was a woman with me and she asked me if I had any prayer that I would say going into the graveyard, and I said that I hadn't …

'Stand there a while,' she said.

'What special prayer is there?' I said, 'but to pray for them as everyone does.'

'Wait there awhile and I'll tell it to you.'

And I did.

'This is the right prayer to say,' she said, 'when you put your foot in through the gate: 'God and Mary be with you. You were as we are, and we will be as you are.'

'Say that always,' she said, 'and I have it from good authority.'

## 20. Women from Kilcatherine buried in Kerry
There used be women in Kilcatherine who settled in Kerry – young girls. They used to marry there, and I never heard of any of them being brought back over to bury them when they died.

## 21. The clothes of the dead
I was present when an old woman who was east in a little shanty asked the priest: 'Wisha Father, I wonder if I will get my clothes if they are sent after me when I die?'

'Oh, I don't know,' he said, 'but you better put them on you. The best thing for you to do is to wear them yourself before you die, in case you wouldn't get them,' said he.

There were people in America from this place who died, and they were seen, but it was before my time.

[There was a man, and] his brother saw a boy [who was dead] ... it isn't far from this place either, and he recognised him. He told his mother. She went to Castletownbere the same day and she bought a suit of clothes for him, made in the shop, and the first Sunday that he [the brother] brought them to Mass – he brought them on three Sundays to Mass – and the first Sunday, that night, he saw him [the dead boy] at the house and the clothes on him. And he had no hat on him, and no hat was sent after him, because he seldom wore one.

She went that day (the mother) and she bought the hat for him, and it was sent after him, and his father saw him somewhere after that and he was wearing the hat. Maybe things are good with them on the other side with God's help.

He saw him beside the house the first time – the brother – and he coming from a walk, and he only had drawers and a shirt on him. He told his mother and his mother was at him for not speaking to him ...

'Did you know him?' said she.

'I did well,' said he. 'Why wouldn't I know him?' said he.

There were people in America before I left Kilcatherine, and I a little child, and they used to write home telling their people to send the clothes with them [after their death].

There was a boy there and he wrote home to his mother and said to her that his brother had died and that he used to see the brother and that he had no hat or braces on him, and to buy him a pair of braces and a hat.

She came to Kilcatherine then – she was living west in Cathair Caim – the sister who got the news about the clothes, and she came to Kilcatherine to her mother and father. She went to Kilcatherine. And she going up to the house, through the field leading up to the house – the path that they used to go up – she heard the coughing and the coughing. She looked around her and she didn't see anybody. And it wasn't the dead man who was talking to her (the man who died beyond) but a brother of hers who was long in the ground before that. It was herself I heard saying it. Right. The coughing, the coughing was beside her going up the field, and she stopped in the place she thought the coughing was coming from. She spoke out boldly: 'Is that you Batt?' said she.

'Upon my word,' said he, 'it's about time you spoke! When you go in now,' said he, 'tell my father to buy a pair of braces and a hat for me, and I won't bother you anymore.'

He wasn't in America but seven days when he (Batt) was killed, and it's drilling he was. Where was he put only in a place which was being drilled already, and the fuse didn't work for them or the powder. And he and another man who had no knowledge of it were sent [working there], and it blasted (the blast exploded) and they were blown into the air.

*Tadhg Ó Murchú*: How were the clothes sent with the soul of the person who died?

*Peig Minihane*: I saw it done, and I did it myself, because three or four went from me.

They put the amount of clothes that would be worn every Sunday – you know, their new clothes, or whatever kind they were, but that they should not be too bad – they put them on a chair inside the door, every one of them – the whole suit together – and they put them out on a chair and shake the holy water on the clothes, and put them outside the door when the sun is going down – the night coming on them. They bring them in then and put them below or above the door (of the kitchen) and leave them there then until morning. Put them outside the door then for nine or ten minutes in the morning. Bring them in the door then and take them up together in your lap, and whatever person is to wear them should come outside the door on his two knees and ask for them first …

'Give them to me in God's name so that he will have them (the dead person's name is mentioned) in eternity.'

The person who has the clothes goes on his knees too, while they are being given to him. They are brought to Mass then, and holy water is shaken on them then in the church. They are bringing them in bundles to the church now …

'For the Last Day', the old people used to say: they liked to send the clothes with their souls.

## 22. Sending things after a child

*Tadhg Ó Murchú*: Did you ever hear that a little pan or a little saucepan used be put in the coffin with a child when it had died? *Peig Minihane*: They were stopped at the coffin, wisha (from putting them in the coffin), but a little pan would be put out on the ditch together with whatever little garments they would have (that the child would be wearing). Máire Ní Mhurchú used to say: 'Ah, he or she is drinking the water with his palms' (for want of the child having a little pan in the other world).

I saw that done in Kilcatherine long before I left it. Máire Ní Mhurchú used to say to them to put it out on the ditch (the little pan) on Saturday night or Sunday morning, and to throw the holy water on it (the little garments of clothes too, I suppose).

## 23. The wedding suit being worn at a funeral

If there was a married couple and one of them died, if it happened that it was in the house that the man would have died, well the woman then, they used to say that, when her husband was being buried, she should put on the suit she had on her the day she was married. I saw that: I heard that, and I saw it done, and I saw the woman who did it.

## 24. The hair in eternity

They used to say that everyone would have to collect their own hair in eternity, and when they would put them in the hole [grave], they wouldn't allow any two who were in the one belly[3] to be put together in the hole – a separate hole for each of them.

'Ah,' said she, 'let one of them go east and the other west – let them go where they like (with the hair).'
An old woman said that, because everyone would have to collect their own hair in eternity, or they would be bald, and there would be a danger when one who went [died] lacked hair, that he would bring another man with him.

## 25. The bones of the dead

There was a man west there at the Bridge *(Droichead a' Chapaill)*[4] and he was being buried in the graveyard, and the boy who is here, my son Micheál, there were bones sticking out of the grave, and he put every bone of them together. The wife of the (dead) man was looking at him collecting the bones and putting them together. Right. When the corpse was put down then he had them together and he threw them with his two hands in with the coffin. Right. When the priest was gone and the people scattered, the woman threw herself on her two knees – the wife of the man who was buried – and it was a terror the amount of prayers she said for him – on account of him [Michael] being so careful about the bones, you know.

### 26. Attracting the water
Oh, that was a belief they had too (the last person to be buried in the graveyard that the water would be drawn to him).

## DEALINGS BETWEEN LIVING AND DEAD

### 1. A woman whose sister came back to her
There was a [dead] woman long ago up there and she said: 'Don't come here so late again any other night,' said she.

'There are many with me now,' said she, but you can't see them. We are going to go down now.'

'It's often a person would have to be out late,' she (the living woman) said.

'It is no harm if you are about any business, but if you are not, be inside on your own hearth at ten o'clock,' she said – she was her sister who had died before that. 'Wherever you are,' said she, 'be inside on your own hearth at ten o'clock, and it's no harm for you to be out before that.'

### 2. The beetle heard at night
In the river west here (behind the house) it used to be heard – the beetle being worked in the river – Gurteen River. Oh, they often heard it – men coming home from seining late at night – they used to hear the beetle, and when they used to come west there right over the water (then) they used not hear a thing.

## STRENGTH AND GREAT DEEDS

*A very strong woman*

I saw them. I know of a woman who was alive at that time who brought a big twenty stone bag (of meal) with her. Well, I saw a woman who brought one of those bags from Eyeries to Kilcatherine: I suppose she brought it a mile, to be right accurate about it; the bag on her back and a rope around her waist as a support for her back. Oh, she was big and strong: the people had enormous strength at that time.

---

1 A woman who had a public house in Kenmare.
2 As a joke she said this – Tadhg Ó Murchú.
3 Twins, in my opinion – or two brothers too I suppose. I didn't think of asking her which – Tadhg Ó Murchú.
4 'Horse Bridge'.

# NATURE

PLANTS

*Woods in olden times*
Did anyone tell you during your travels … you know where
Colleros School is, from there west to Ardgroom Bridge, well,
there was a forest growing in all of that, from the schoolhouse to
the bridge that is west in the village, there was a forest growing
in all that long ago. Well, a man went from the east – the most
easterly tree – to the tree in the west, walking from tree to tree
without his foot touching the ground. His feet never came onto
the ground until he came to *Droichead a' Chapaill*, and there was
no one of those trees, they said, but that its roots were underground in Ardgroom.

   Oh, they had to be cut, because they were short of firing:
they had no place to cut turf.

MAMMALS

*1. Tree cats and wild cats*
They were in Kilcatherine, down under the graveyard, by the
sea. There was a thicket there and the place was full of them.
They set fire to the thicket and that finished them – the tree cats.
*Erú*, my dear, your life would be in danger from them. Some of
them used to call them wild cats. The tree cats were worse than
the wild cats, they used say. A dog would frighten the wild cat,
but the tree cat would have no fear of it.

*2. The fox*
I heard that some man who was east there in Colleros went
looking for a man with a gun who was in the area so that he

would fire a shot into the den – the fox's den. The fox used be doing damage on him. But the man came and he fired a shot into the den and he (the man with the gun) did not sleep that night, nor the following night, nor the night after that, nor for a week. And he used be falling asleep and 'twas dreaming about the fox he used be – screeching like the fox. But his mother made some cure for him after that.

INSECTS

*The devil's coach horse*
It would be no use for you to kill the devil's coach horse without taking its head off with your teeth. I saw a girl doing it and she is still alive – she is a little old woman now.

Seven deadly sins (removed from your soul if you killed it): you would have no sin on you then. I suppose it was only talk!

'Iné, iné, iné,' said the devil's coach horse.

# FOLK-MEDICINE

### 1. Ivy for a burn

For a child who was burned, ivy was always their cure. You would boil it well too, and you would put it on the burn. It had to be growing in a place where there would be no view of the sea.

### 2. Camomile (i)

They used to pull it in a place where it was long – it used to be that length, the camomile – in a place where it would be growing on good rich ground.

They used to leave it drying out on the cliffs and I saw it being saved and, my heart to the Lord, I never handled a bit of it. When they had it saved, dry, they used put it on nails on the roof beams: they used tie it with a cord.

They used put it drawing then and when you would put your head in the door you would get its smell inside the house – the camomile. They used be boiling it and drinking it. The tinkers used be making saucepans at that time and they used put it drawing in the saucepan. It used be good for a person with the 'decay'[1] – you would take it and leave it wither under the sun.

### 3. Camomile (ii)

What they used do with the camomile, they used pull it and save it well and hang it under the beam (under a beam in the kitchen), and then when it was needed, or any neighbour (had need) for it, you would boil it and wash the head with the water from it in the morning before you would eat any breakfast. And they were very grateful to it, anyone who tried it, no doubt (as a cure for headache).

### 4. Cabbage
In the middle of the head of cabbage was the cure for headache.

### 5. Liocán
You would skin it – you would heat it and soften it on the fire, and put the side of it that had faced the sun to the wound.

### 6. Plantain
I don't know if you knew Mrs Mehigan in Kenmare. I was with her one night – I slept there. I was east there doing a journey[2] on 15 August. She was related to the man of this house. And that was the night that none of us fell asleep. But she said that there was no sickness (wound or disease) that ever came on the people but that the cure for it was growing in the soil.

If you cut your finger, the best cure (poultice) that you ever put on it – anything you could cut using a sharp edge – and the way you would go about it, would be to go out and pull a fistful of plantain that used to be growing in the grass and bring it in. You would have to – if you were cut today – you would have to pull it fresh again tomorrow. You would cut a little tuft then in the morning, she said, from the amount you brought in, and chew it in your mouth. That was the cure of the plantain. And you would put a little bit – the size of your finger – on fresh butter, mixed all through it. My hand and my word on it that it would be a bad cut that wouldn't be healed in three days; that there would be no fear of it from then on; but that the badness would be gone.

### 7. Cniubh
It was in the mountain it used to be found. The boys used be picking it, and it was in the east of Eyeries parish that it grew, up in the mountain. But they used be picking it and giving it away – the boys – and it died out. I never saw it.

### 8. Comfrey
He was west there in Canfie (a man), and it [the comfrey] used be a cure for farsey in horses, and he had a very lame horse – three of its legs were lame – and he came here for the comfrey.

He took away the roots and the man of this house wasn't in at all: he was mad because he took away so much of it – [saying] that it was many a person who would want it for a hundred reasons.

Well, any sore you would have – they used not have any shoes on them (the people at that time) – you would cut it (the comfrey) and there would be that length of root on it, and they used take it then and clean it as clean (as anything that was ever cleaned). And there used be a fine black layer (of bark) on the outside of it and they used to remove that. And you would scrape the white (stuff) then with a knife, and it would be like glue: it would stick to your fingers. Well, you would take it then and put it to whatever was sore and it would stick to the sore place until it healed. Oh, there's great healing in the comfrey, no doubt.

### 9. Luibh na hAbha [the Herb of the River]
It used be west there (growing) in the river – a dark brown colour – and any sepsis that would be in the house, the mother of the one who would have anything like that, sepsis or a carbuncle, the mother would pull this from the stones. And the person who would have the sepsis would have to leave the house – clear out of the house. It would be put into a cabbage leaf and put under the embers – it would be put into the fire softening. Oh, I saw it (done) but, thanks be to God, I never did it (myself) because I never needed to. *Luibh na hAbha* [the Herb of the River] they used call it – dark brown: it wasn't completely black at all. I saw it.

### 10. Garlic
But there was a thing growing … did you ever hear of the garlic? It is still done here. In the neck I saw it put – a little hole would be made in the neck with a penknife (in the calf's neck – the skin would be pierced). A little slit would be put in it – the skin would be cut and the garlic put in as if it was growing. I heard old people saying during my time that there was no better cure in Ireland than the garlic.

### 11. Bad luck connected with herbs
I heard people say that you should not use any kind of herbs; that it is not lucky at all to use them.

## 12. Wildfire (ruacht)

Wildfire they used to call that – the *ruacht*. They used have the blood of a black cat to prevent it. They used put a slit in the cat's ear and squeeze out the blood on a saucer, and dip a little rag in the blood and use it to stop this, or write down their names.

## 13. Soil from the priest's tomb

*Tadhg Ó Murchú*: Did you ever hear that people used to take soil with them from the tomb of a priest who was buried in the grave-yard, as a cure for sores?

*Peig Minihane*: Indeed I did, and I saw it done too – the soil being taken from the tomb and being put on something sore. *Uaigh an tSagairt* [the Priest's Grave], it is west in Kilcatherine, and the priest is buried in the corner of the ruin – in the south-east corner of the ruin – and many came and took the soil with them and they were satisfied (grateful for it). You would have to put back the soil again.

## 14. A cure in the soil from under hazel

There is a tree – it is growing in many places – that there is a cure in the soil from under it – hazel. They used take the soil away with them, and … I don't know that, if they used put it back. I don't think they used to put back the soil. But I heard a woman, who was over there, saying that she brought it with her: some kind of sore came on her knee, and old people asked if there was any hazel tree around anywhere, and she came to this tree and took the soil with her and she was very satisfied with it.

## 15. Leeching

I remember a boy who went into service in a big shop where meal and flour were sold, west there in Eyeries – he was a son of my father's brother – a young boy – and he was injured putting some load up in a loft.

But he was injured on the stairs going up with the bag of meal on his back, and he had to give up. His head was hurt and he had to give up, and it was a brother of mine he sent on his own behalf looking for the shopkeeper.

But he got very sick and he had to go to hospital, and if he did, he was sick and well sick. A foreign ship came into the harbour – into Kilcatherine Harbour – and the ship was there for a while so that he heard tell of (a sailor who was on the ship), and he asked his father if there was any doctor on board the ship who would do him any good: the man of the house knew him (the boy's father). Right. His father went looking for this man who was in the ship, that he had heard about, that he was better than any doctor (and he told him his story) …

'Have you him at home?' said this man from the ship.

'I haven't,' said he. 'He is in hospital in Castletown.'

'I declare to the world!' he said, 'that I'll go to see him,' said he. 'I'm going to Castletown tomorrow.'

He was sorry for the creature – for the poor father. He went to see him and he saw him, and his head, they said, would not fit into a keg, it was so changed. On his instructions, then, he ordered that he be taken out of the bed and put on a table. That happened when I was a little one. He was put on a table for him and he took a box out of his pocket, and what was in the box but a worm which was alive, [according to] the people who saw it.

The worm was put … a plate was put under his head and he put the worm on the plate, and he rubbed something to his face (to the boy's face), and he endured it, the poor man, and it was hard for him. He was left there until the worm drew a quart of blood from the side of his head, I heard. And when the worm would fill itself it would come out onto the plate and leave the blood on the plate. But he recovered well after that (the boy).

*Tadhg Ó Murchú*: But did you ever hear of any man who used to take blood from people?

*Peig Minihane*: I didn't know of anyone like that around the place, or if there was I didn't hear it.

### 16. Bleeding animals
It was from the rump of the tail they used to take the blood from the animals, and they used to cut their ears. They used to do that before the calves would get the sickness. I saw a man doing it – a man who was able to do it – and they were very grateful to him.

### 17. The serpent's knot – a cure for blackleg
There was a woman, she was west there on the side of the road.

She was there as large as life, God's blessing on her soul – Máire O'Connell she was called, after her husband, but she was of the Lowney family when she was young. They had a shop. I saw her do it. Nine knots she used to put on the cord against the fur ('against the hair,' too they say – 'against the grain') – against the fur that used to be growing on their calves, you know. She used to start at the rump.

*Tadhg Ó Murchú*: How used she make the knot?

*Peig Minihane*: There was nothing to do but to catch hold of it. She used to hold the two ends of the cord and whatever she used to do with the knots, she used put the end of the cord through them, and upon my word, I saw the calf (that she did it to) getting up.

*Ceathrú Ghorm* [Blackleg] they used to call that disease. I never saw any man doing it anyway, but I saw her doing it – [for] anyone who was living near her.

*Tadhg Ó Murchú*: Used she be brought to the house to do it?

*Peig Minihane*: (They used to, but) no horse or cart used be brought to her. Oh, she cured many animals.

It (blackleg) used not come on any animal only a good animal – a yearling calf. It wouldn't come on the miserable thing or the poor thing anyway ...

'Don't be good to your calf until it is over a year old,' the old people used to say.

### 18. A cure for warts (i)

That used to be a cure for the warts. You would count all the warts on your legs or hands and you would get the same number of little pebbles then, and put them into a paper and fold the paper around them and put them in the middle of the road. The first person who would come the road then and take up the paper, he [the person with the warts] was rid of the warts and they would grow on that person.

### 19. A cure for warts (ii)

They used have that as a cure too, for the warts – the froth from the potato water. When the potatoes would be boiling – when they would be starting to boil – you would gather the froth and rub it to them. It would rot them.

### 20. A cure for headache

A relative of mine gave (me as a cure) before that, on May Morning, before the sun would come up, to go out and bend down on the nearest green field to the door and tear three mouthfuls (of the green grass) with my teeth, and chew it, and swallow it (that it would cure a headache). But I had promised [to go on] the journey east (in Kenmare).

That was a cure for headache (to go out on May Morning, etc.) and the person who would do that, no thread would get tangled on them either but would become untangled. It used to be awkward too, the thread made from the flax. But I did it for the headache, and I was thankful to it no doubt, to tell you the truth.

### 21. An unusual cure for toothache

If you came across a pig around the house or anywhere, and saw it – it's often we saw [one] – scratching its behind on the ground, you would lie on the ground (and) put your head down on it – in the place where you would have seen the pig scratching its behind. You would make the Sign of the Cross with your mouth on the place, across, over and back, and you would never again get a toothache.

### 22. Pulling teeth long ago

*Tadhg Ó Murchú*: Who used to pull the people's teeth here long ago?
*Peig Minihane*: Oh, they would pull them for one another. They used put a cord of fishing line on them. You would be outside then and you would lean with all your strength on the cord, pulling it.
*Tadhg Ó Murchú*: What used be done with the tooth that would be pulled?
*Peig Minihane*: You would put a little bit of the 'angel'[3] with it and throw it over your right shoulder – I didn't hear any prayer being said – to grow them back again. I didn't see it in Kilcatherine at all (the angel being thrown with the tooth), but here – the angel.

### 23. The blood charm

The man that I had here had the blood charm, God's blessing on his soul, and I saw him do it. He was here, one time, and he left in a new spade to go working with it, he left it standing out there by the wall, to bring it with him when he would be going working. We had a little girl here with us who was four years old. The child went out – she was four years – after the spade being left in. She was outside, and when he came in, she ran in after him covered in blood. She knocked the spade and she got a prod of the spade up under the nose and it cut her well too. The old woman who was here in the house was still alive – my husband's mother:

'Have you the blood charm?' she said to the son. 'I heard you had.'

He brought her to the door and he put the charm on her and the bleeding stopped immediately.

### 24. *A green sod to stop bleeding*
If you were to dig a green sod and put the green side to the cut it would stop the blood.

### 25. *Moss to stop bleeding*
They used to use moss too to stop bleeding.

### 26. *Father Larkin and the bone woman*
Father Larkin (a parish priest who was in Eyeries), his horse got its head, and if it did, it knocked him off its back and something in his shoulder was broken. Well, he walked from here, I suppose to the north of Ireland – it was in Eyeries that the priests were living – to doctors, and he met no doctor in his travels who did him any good, and his shoulder was not healing.

There was a woman in Kilcatherine, the mother of the priest's clerk, and it's many a good plaster she made, and it's many a bad thing she healed too. She herself made the plaster and gave it to her son – he was the clerk – and she said to him to bring that to him and to put it to his shoulder, and to keep it there as long as he could. And she didn't have hardly any of the stuff to make it: she would have to have everything needed to make it. She made the plaster – as much as she had of it – and she put it into a paper that had no ink on it (no sign of ink – clean white paper). That cured the priest, and you may say that the priest payed her well! It healed the shoulder, the plaster she made.

## 27. A journey to Old Kenmare – a cure for an eye disease

There was a man east there and he was married for the third time and he had two girls (when the third wife died on him), and he had one of those churns that had a wheel on them (a barrel churn). But he used to make the churning himself and when it used be done he used send one of the girls here to me, calling me to take the butter from the churn. But one of them came here late one evening calling me – they were at the churning east – and I went off east with her. But my eldest daughter came with me – she went east with me to keep me company coming back. But when I had taken the butter from the churn …

'Come on now,' I said to my daughter, ''tis about time for us [to] go home – the door will be closed on us.' The talk about journeys[4] reminded me of this now.

Well, we headed for home and the night was so quiet that you would think there wasn't a puff of wind from the air, no doubt. And the two of us came west, shoulder to shoulder.[5] As we were coming west just where the scout[6] is east there, well, a breeze of wind came and I imagined that it blew all the dust that was on the road into my eyes and it took away my sight.

Well, a woman who was west here – a woman friend of mine – was advising me that the day of the journey [to Old Kenmare] was upon us. I couldn't see anything – in the place where there was a cow out there, I used imagine that there were two cows there. Well, I went to Kenmare on the fourteenth of August: I went and did my journey to Kenmare. I went up to the graveyard.

Well, when we were coming west after doing the journey – it was a horse and cart we had – it was a man from this place who was doing the journey east who had brought me and the other woman east to Kenmare. On our way home from Kenmare in the evening after doing the journey I could see a crow up in Cuhig[7] and I couldn't see the side of the road on my way east.

---

1 Miner's Consumption – as a result of breathing the dry silicate dust of the mines. The miners' lungs became scarred and this made them very prone to infections like T.B. Many miners came home from Butte, Montana suffering from the 'decay'.

2 On a pilgrimage, doing 'rounds' etc.

3 Embers from the fire – See p. 88

4 Pilgrimages

5 The neighbour's house was only a short distance east from her – Tadhg Ó Murchú.

6 A little stream of water a short distance east of the house – Tadhg Ó Murchú.

7 A townland that is east up from Gurteen – Tadhg Ó Murchú.

# DIVISION OF TIME,
# FESTIVALS AND PILGRIMAGES

*The Cross Day of the Year*
The Cross Day of the Year, they did not like to start anything at all, even the setting of the garden. That was the fourth day after Christmas Day.

THE COMMON FESTIVALS

*1. Shrove Night and the Skellig Lists[1]*
The horns used be blown before the night would come at all. It's often we used say that there wouldn't be any horn on any cow on Shrove Night.

Oh, they used say it, that they would have to go to the Skellig, anyone who would not marry.

They used be gathering bottles for a fortnight before the night – a big bottle – and they used put a drop of water into the bottle and a cork in it, and leave it down on a fire that wouldn't be too hot. And the bottom would come out of it then, and they would have the bottle as a horn.

*Erú*, a gang of them would come then – (to the house) of any girl or youth who wasn't married, you know – and you would think they would take the roof off the house: they used not come to any other house but to them.

The Skellig List, it was here too.

*2. Good Friday*
That's what they used say anyway, that you would not sow anything on Good Friday only something you would not harvest

71

again that year. To sow anything was forbidden no doubt. They would go to the strand and gather seaweed, but they wouldn't do any spadework (on Good Friday). The limpets and 'bright gathering', they used bring them [home] with them. The bright gathering is a particular type of thing that used have a shell on it – cockles and *biorlacans*.

### 3. *Patrick's cross*

Everyone would be given a twig and they used do it themselves (to cross themselves with the twig). It was no use for you to put the Patrick's Day cross on yourself except with a sally that was growing. You would put the tip of it in the fire and light it, and then quench it, and make the cross on your forearm – of your right hand. Everyone would do it for himself, as I remember anyway.

### 4. *Easter Sunday*

'Egg Sunday' no doubt. They used make more of Egg Sunday than of Christmas Night. No man or woman, nor any boy or girl used eat any egg during the year only on Easter Sunday: times were poor God help us. Every man would get six eggs on Easter Sunday, and the women and girls, four, and they would not eat them with bread at all, only with the potatoes; they used have the potatoes in, ready for the morning to eat them with the eggs. I remember that well from when I was a child.

### 5. *The signs of summer*

> Holly and hazel,
> Elder and rowan,
> Shimmering bright ash
> From the mouth of the ford.

Even so, it's not those they have everywhere, because they don't have them growing. Before sunrise, before the sun will rise (the summer is brought in). Oh, it's many a person used bring them in and go to sleep again – maybe I did it myself. They used put them between the boards of the loft and the beam and they used leave them there for a year (the green boughs).

*Tadhg Ó Murchú*: What used they do with them then after the year?
*Peig Minihane*: Oh, throw them out. Yes, or throw them in the fire
if they fell down.

## 6. May Eve
I saw them lighting the boughs and going among the cows – we
had that as a custom ourselves on May Eve – they would be thrown
among the cows, where they stood. Oh I don't know what the
basis for it was.

## 7. Saint John's Eve
*Tadhg Ó Murchú*: I suppose ye used to have the bonfire here on
Saint John's Eve.
*Peig Minihane*: We used to, a fire they don't have now, wisha. The
Saint John's Eve fire, whatever the basis for it was? *Erú*, they
used have a big *láthair*[2] and they gathering for a week, and the
thing that stopped it, there used be small children and they were
afraid that their clothes would catch fire. There was a big *láthair*
that had the width of the field in it – a big wide level *cnocán*[3] –
west in Kilcatherine, and it's there we used have the fire.

Oh, everyone gathering (to it) for a week, and maybe a fortnight. Those (customs) are all stamped out now, dear.
*Tadhg Ó Murchú*: What fuel used they gather?
*Peig Minihane*: Oh *erú*, big bushes of furze that used be cut beforehand by them for a long time – maybe a month – that used
be rusty-red then: it was easy to set fire to them – that used be
growing on the ditches, and bundles of hay and straw from the
gardens. It was mostly furze they used have: they used cut it beforehand. A bonfire, we used to call it. The old people used say
to the young people: 'Are ye gathering for the bonfire – for Saint
John's Eve?'

I heard it said (that they used put an animal's bone in the
fire), but nothing was put in it as I remember only the furze, and
it's often they were given dire warnings on account of taking the
boughs from the gaps on the cows.
*Tadhg Ó Murchú*: Was anyone chosen to light the fire?
*Peig Minihane*: Nobody was chosen, but when the sun used be
just gone down, they used bring a bucket of fire with them from

the houses around. They used make a turf fire first, beside the big fire, and when the time used come to light it, then the gang used gather and they used be throwing it on top of it as fast as their hands could do it. I declare to the world that the old people used to come looking at them – on the *cnocáns*, you know.

*Tadhg Ó Murchú*: I suppose ye used have fun around the fire.

*Peig Minihane*: Oh fun, that then surely, too! They used be threatening the young people that they would throw them into the flames if they wouldn't keep out from the fire; they used be afraid that their clothes would catch fire, and they would too. Oh they used have fun no doubt, and lots coming looking at them too, married people.

*Tadhg Ó Murchú*: They used have a dance I suppose.

*Peig Minihane*: Oh a dance – It wasn't any 'high gates' they used have at all, as they used call the steps, but hornpipes, and it's they were the fine dancers.

*Tadhg Ó Murchú*: Used they have the 'country dance'?

*Peig Minihane*: Yes. Yes. They used have it all right – the country dance.

*Tadhg Ó Murchú*: What used they do when the fire went out?

*Peig Minihane*: Oh, when it would be going out, they used go off then, and go to houses and they used have a dance – 'puss music'. They used have some fun around the fire, dancing and singing (the young people).

## 8. Hallowe'en

'At Hallowe'en, put a tether on your calf', said the man long ago. To his son he said it: he was dying and he was giving him advice.

It's often we heard it, that it wasn't right for the men or the women to do anything (on Hallowe'en) only praying, that they, the holy souls, used be on the beams watching the prayers. Oh, they used have games here too, putting apples in the water tub. It's many a wetting I saw the boys in this house getting (from doing it). It's not that they do now but to hang it from a nail and catch it with your mouth. (Long ago) the nail used be put in the apple to push it down under the water – a good thick nail. It used be pushed into it, in such a way, you know, that you could not grip it at all.

### 9. The Christmas Block

Did you ever hear any chat going on about the Christmas Block? Oh, it was here (as a custom). I put it in the fire myself too when I heard the chat going on about it. Any piece at all (of wood) – bog deal, it would be as good as a block, even if it was only the length of your shoe. You would leave it lighting and put it outside then and leave it outside until it was cold, cold, cold.

They used bring it in then and leave it up under the beams, and leave it there for a year, and with the grace of God, no house that would have it in it would catch fire.

That's how it was, wisha, no doubt. Some little twig – a short little bog deal twig used be put (in the fire on Christmas Night). They used leave it go out then.

### 10. Christmas candles

*Tadhg Ó Murchú*: And wasn't it forbidden to quench any candle that would be lit on Christmas Night – but to leave it burn out? *Peig Minihane*: That was forbidden here too, wisha, no doubt. Oh, since I came here it's often I used put the candle in the middle of the floor and leave it lighting there until morning.

### 11. Saint Stephen's Day

Well, I don't know how it was in Castletown, because I wasn't there, but in Eyeries they used have a drum and music on Saint Stephen's Day. There used be twelve in the gang on Saint Stephen's Day, and ivy on all of them. A horse came here and you couldn't see any bit of it (a man on a saddled horse). He had the horse dressed up in holly and ivy, going from door to door and three or four others with him – little boys – and no house left him off without giving him a shilling.

There was a parish priest, he was in Eyeries on Saint Stephen's Day one time, and the activity and music was going on, and he was standing at the church gate looking at them – Father Larkin – and he came out from the door, out onto the road and he walked up. There was a little height there. He went up onto the level, and you may say that he danced a bout of a hornpipe as cleverly as I ever saw it, the parish priest, and he gave them a half-crown then.

*12. The Night of the Three Kings*
Look, Little Christmas Night – did you ever hear anything about
it?

> The Night of the Three Kings
> Wine is made from the water,
> And the pin from the holly,
> And silk from the tuft.

At the hour of midnight, when the night and day are parting (that
happens).

It's often I heard people saying, before I ever came to Ardgroom, that two people went watching at that time of night –
two young boys – and they brought vessels with them for the
water, when the water would be wine, and it is said that they
were never seen since.

It was the old people who were alive long ago who said that.

And isn't it some work, the old people who were here before us – they used to go down to Waterford digging the potatoes. God love them, they didn't have anything else. And it's
more honour they used give to Little Christmas Night (than to
Big Christmas Night): they used not give any respect to Big Christmas Night only to the Night of the Three Kings – the people below [in Waterford].


LOCAL FESTIVALS, PATTERNS AND PILGRIMAGES

*1. The three tussocks in Loch a' Coinleáin*[4]
A soldier of war came, they came ashore east in Kenmare, I heard,
and they came looking at it (at *Loch a' Coinleáin*). I suppose he
wasn't a Catholic, the soldier. There were six of them there. On
Easter Sunday morning it was. Journeys used be done there at that
time too and they are being done still, but I suppose there aren't
very many (doing them now) compared to the number that used
to.

There's no Easter Sunday morning, before sunrise, that the
three tussocks don't do their course around the lake, and anyone

doing the journey while these are going around (it used be said) that it was a good journey.

What did one of the soldiers do, when the tussocks came around, but to take out his pistol and he stuck it down – whatever thing (weapon) he had in his hand – and the blood went around the lake, and the water was dark red for years after that.

They used go under water before that, the sick people – they used be put under the water, keeping a grip on them. But it's not done at all now.[5]

The tussocks are lame ever since, and late in the evening, after the sun has gone down, they leave their positions and do their course around the lake.

## 2. Counting the rounds on the journey (i)

You would take up the pebbles (little stones – ten of them) in the place you would be doing the journey. You would start the prayers then.

You will take up ten (pebbles). You will throw (away) one of them then (in the place where you start the journey), and you will keep the nine. And you will go around then with the nine and you will be throwing one away all the time, as you go around.

## 3. Counting the rounds on the journey (ii)

There is a journey done in Kenmare, and when you go into the graveyard, you'll go this distance east as far as that ruin there east before you come to the right spot.[6] I did the journey a couple of times. (You will have) ten pebbles: you will be throwing away one where you are (in the place you start) and you will be going around until you have the ten (the other nine) used up.

## 4. The Kenmare journey

*Tadhg Ó Murchú*: When is this journey in Kenmare?

*Peig Minihane*: The 15 August – Our Lady's Day in autumn. There is a wall down at the top of the strand. You would go out through a narrow little gate at the top of the strand. The well is on your right hand side, and a little canopy over it, and there used be a cup there most of the time so that the people could take a drink.

There used often be a man there guiding the people who didn't know the place (directing them).

This man used to say to us that it was no use if you didn't have the journey done before the sun went down; that there would be no benefit for you in the business.

The journey was very good; a lame old man who was there said: 'This is a good journey, with the help of God, and be careful about your prayers.' He had a crutch and a walking stick. But there was a priest's grave where we were doing the journey, and there was another grave behind it that had a man's hand (on it), and the five fingers standing up straight, and it was not revealed whether it was a priest or a saint. And I genuflected in front of that: we were told that – to genuflect to that as we went around.

There was a good round there – nine rounds. I went there with a headache, and I went there and did my journey, and I thank God that I didn't get it since.

*Tadhg Ó Murchú*: What prayers did you say when you were doing the Kenmare Journey?

*Peig Minihane*: The Rosary – a decade going around – and there is a place there, where you would start and go on your knees.

There was a woman from Colleros down there some time, and she asked a man who was there: 'What prayers are said, please, going around here?'

'The Rosary,' said he.

But that's how it was.


### 5. Lady's Well

There's another place there, then, when you would come down the street (the street of Kenmare) – two miles from the Sound Bridge, at the northern end of the street – which they call Lady's Well. That wasn't done up at all when I was going there. Well, a dry year came when no water came into the well (and) on the morning of this day that the journey was being done there, there was water in the well, and there were vessels – cups – there for everyone to take a drink out of the well.

On the morning of this day, the first person who came to do the journey there – the well was dry – was a girl and she told the man who did the place up that the well was dry.

He gave them two buckets – two girls – and he told them to bring two buckets of spring water from another well. And when they came to the (holy) well the water was there before them in the well! Another journey used be done then (at Lady's Well) after doing the journey above (the Kenmare Journey).

There was a woman there one evening (at Lady's Well) – it was said that she was from North Kerry – and she had no English, only Irish.

I was there myself, early in the evening, and she had prayers that I never heard (the likes of) before in my life, in Irish. She had a cup of water in her hand while she was saying the prayers, and when she began she said: 'I will say the Prayer of Our Saviour now for ye, people, and the Glorious Mother.'

She gave the basis for it too (the prayer), but I didn't bring it with me [remember it]. Oh, my bitter sorrow, and she was well worth putting saying it too … a three-cornered shawl on her, and two hankies and one on her neck and the other on her head, colourful, silk – the one she had on her bonnet.

I declare to the world, if you were never on a journey, it would do you good to go and listen to the prayers they had – anyone who would have the courage to say them.

Oh, she had Irish, make no mistake!

### 6. Gobnait's Day

Did you hear any account of Gobnait's Day? There were masons building a new house in Cathair Caim that time: 'Today is Gobnait's Day,' said one of the men. 'I won't put any stone in any house – it isn't right to build any wall.'

Oh, the man of the house and the rest of them spoke. They said that he was going somewhere else and that he wanted to stop the work. They used work then, if it was autumn, before they had any breakfast.

But they were arguing about the day anyway, about going to work on the day, and they went in to their breakfast and when they came out there wasn't a stone in the wall that was built – they were building it a fortnight before that – there wasn't a stone they had put in the house but was knocked down to the foundation when they came out. It's often I heard them talking about that – it's often no doubt.

'Right, now,' said the man who was trying not to go to work, 'right, now,' said he, 'there is no other name for these days only holy days.'

### 7. The boundary journey

I had decided to do the journey before I heard about this (the cure): and they say that if you decide to do a journey, you should do it before you die. And many used be doing the journey to the boundary waters – the boundary of the two counties – between the two counties. I did that with a sore breast I had.

*Tadhg Ó Murchú*: But how did you do the boundary journey – could you tell me every move you made on the journey – if you don't mind?

*Peig Minihane*: I'll tell you (as) I was told and as I myself did it. You would leave your house and you wouldn't talk to a living person – if you met the priest or the pope – no word to any living person from when you would put your foot over the threshold. You would go out and go to the place where there was a river (or a stream) between the two counties – and go down on the strand to the high tide mark. You would go on your two knees then at the high tide mark, and the water coming down to it from the river. You would say five prayers then – five 'Our Father Who Art in Heaven', five 'Hail Marys' and five 'Glories', in honour of the water and the journey that was being done, in the hope that it would do you good. You would drink three drops of it with your hands. Well, some of them used bring a little bottle back with them – a little bottle of the water to drink at home.

But some man who heard the story said that the cork should be put in the bottle under the water (the bottle you would have, you should put the cork in it under the water as you took it). Everyone who ever went the way said that the journey had no benefit if you spoke to anyone from the time you left your own threshold until you come back again. That was part of it no doubt. You would decide then to do it three Saturdays and three Sunday mornings – that journey three times. And any devil of a day … I did the journey here when my son was sick, on his behalf – and there wasn't one day of them but a man or a woman met me, and, the devil, didn't I take to the field to get away from them in case they would speak to me – in case I'd break the custom!

## 8. Cnoc na hUlla

West at the Mines in Beara, on Saint Michael's Eve … there is a place that they call *Cnoc na hUlla*. They used to do a journey there on Saint Michael's Eve, and then (again) on the morning of Saint Michael's Day, the following day.

*Tadhg Ó Murchú*: Was there any holy well there?

*Peig Minihane*: Oh, I suppose there was. They used go west there from this place. There used be a big gathering there anyway.

## 9. Ré Eidhneáin

*Ré Eidhneáin,* there use be a journey there on May Day. It is on this (north) side of Castletownbere.

## 10. Ard na hUlla

*Ard na hUlla,* on the north-east side of the harbour (Ballycrovane). I think it was on Saint Brigit's Eve that a journey used be made there, but I'm not sure.

---

1 She didn't have one – or any part of one of the lists – Tadhg Ó Murchú.

2 A site for the fire.

3 A hillock.

4 In the townland of Bunaw, Tuosist Parish, Co. Kerry. A big pattern used be held here on 7 and 8 July to celebrate the feast of Saint Killian.

5 I used hear my father talking about that – big stumps of girls, he said, stripped by their mothers and they ducking them under the water – Tadhg Ó Murchú.

6 A cowshed about forty spade lengths east of the house – Tadhg Ó Murchú.

# POPULAR BELIEF AND MAGIC

### 1. The midwife who had special knowledge

Well, there was a woman west in our place when I was young and she was expecting a child. I'm telling you that some of them had knowledge. When she fell sick with the child the midwife came to her – I guarantee you that it wasn't doctors they had – and when the midwife came in …

'How are you?' she said.

'I'm sick enough,' said she.

Right. I suppose she was sick enough because there were two – twins.

'You have twins,' said she (the midwife), 'and there is a cross against one of them.'

Right. She was born, and she was right – I suppose she was a wisewoman – that it all came true after that. She had a handicapped child.

### 2. Máire Ní Mhurchú and the hare

There was a woman here too – Máire Ní Mhurchú – she was west there in Eyeriesbeg, and it's many a night she spent outside, the poor woman, in the company of the 'good people'. Máire Ní Mhurchú, God's blessing on her soul, she was a great woman. I don't remember her, but I had a brother – the eldest of us – and when he was ten years old, my mother sent him on a message, west through a little hill which was there: that's where the path was. It was an aunt of ours who was there. But she sent the little boy west around ten o'clock (in the day), and the dog followed him – the dog is always following the boys. But the dog followed him anyway. When he had gone a certain distance west he saw the hare coming out of a cliff which was there – *An Fhaill*

*Mhór* [The Big Cliff]. Right. He saw the hare coming out of the cliff and he put the dog after it and the dog caught it and was tearing and ripping it. He went and did his message, where his mother sent him, and he came home, and after dinner, he stretched on the seat and fell asleep. She came in (his mother) and she asked him what was wrong with him and he said that he didn't know.

I suppose she heated milk for him: she couldn't do any more for him. The next day he was bad, and she went out to Eyeries for something for him, and she saw this woman, Máire Ní Mhurchú, but she didn't go to her, but she saw her in Eyeries. My mother went west to the church. She brought a little bottle with her for holy water – maybe she didn't have any of it in [at home] – and she met Máire Ní Mhurchú.

Right …

'Stay there awhile,' said she, 'until I come out of the church.' They knew one another. 'Stay there awhile until I come out of the church,' said Máire Ní Mhurchú to her. 'You have a little boy sick,' said she.

'I have,' said she, 'since yesterday.'

'Ha ha, you have!' said she. 'If you waited until tomorrow you would be too late. And why did he put the dog after the hare?' said she. 'It wasn't a hare that was there but an old woman, and he [your son] is gone from you now,' said she. 'But hurry as fast as ever you can,' said she, 'until you get home.'

But she told her to do something for him for three mornings, and she did. And he improved, and from that day until the day he left Ireland to go to America, he never put any dog after any hare.

*Tadhg Ó Murchú*: How well she knew what happened to the boy!

*Peig Minihane*: She knew it herself: she knew what he did, because she heard it at night when the *trom-mo-lámh*[1] was around her.


### 3. *Máire Ní Mhurchú and the girl who did her water*[2] *in the pot*

About a week after that, there was a young girl in the house – in the same house where this boy was.[3]

She got up (out of bed), late at night, and she came down through the kitchen door from the room and she made her water in the pot, and it was a teapot belonging to the good people who were inside, but she saw nobody.

Right. The girl ... the young girl was pouring out the tea for the company [the good people] who were in the house (and) she [one of the good people] threw a jug at her and the jug went in through her thigh, and no one saw it until Máire Ní Mhurchú took it out – until it troubled her.

Right. Her mother went looking for Máire Ní Mhurchú in the end and she told her her story.

'Ah, don't be telling me at all!' she said. 'You had a black-guard of a daughter and she did that, and she was old enough to understand!' said she. 'She was old enough to understand that she shouldn't do it. But the jug that the woman had making the tea, it's in her thigh and it's hard to get it out too,' said she. She said to the mother then, to go to the nearest flow of water ...

'And there is a herb there,' said she, 'growing there at the side of the river, which is a dark brown colour. Bring a pouch with you,' she said 'of cloth, and pull a nice little fist of it – more than a battered saucepanful of it. And don't leave any signs of it near the house,' she said, 'while you are doing it.'

Right. She said to the mother not to let her [the young girl] inside at all after bringing it in – the herb. She said to her to have two fine big leaves of cabbage inside and to put this herb into the two leaves, and to put the two leaves under the embers, and that nobody, on any account, should look at or disturb the fire in any way, and when the cabbage would be soft, to call her (the daughter) and tell her to come inside and go to bed.

'When she is in the bed then,' she said, 'get a piece of white cloth, put it [the herb] in there and go to her with it and put it to the place where she is sore, and tie strong cloth around it. The jug is breaking up inside in her thigh.'

Right (the mother did as Máire Ní Mhurchú ordered her to do). During the night the girl felt something next to her in the bed, and what was there only the jug – the herb drew it out – and she didn't speak a word until the day came.

'Be praying now, for as long as you live, for Máire Ní Mhur-chú' (said her mother to her). 'You would be in your grave only for her.'

She saw her in the church then after Mass (Máire Ní Mhurchú), and she called her aside …

'Ha, ha!' said she, 'frighten her now,' said she, 'and tell her not to do anything like that ever again: let her have a vessel in the bedroom with her,' said she.

## 4. Máire Ní Mhurchú and the woman who was abducted

The fairy boats were often seen, and this wisewoman who was around the place long ago, she brought a boat from the Kerry side, accompanying them. The wisewoman (Máire Ní Mhurchú) told the woman's husband on the quiet to meet her on a certain night.

'Where will I meet you?' said he.

'Be on the northern side of Puleen Bridge,' said she.

Right, anyway, his wife had been abducted and Máire Ní Mhurchú told him that she would direct him to her.

'We will be in such and such a place,' said she, 'and I will be on the last horse. There will be twenty horses there,' said she – people who were abducted, you know, 'and people riding pillion on them, and leave the rest pass you by,' said she. 'And go to the priest (first) and don't tell anyone anything, and get holy water from him, and bring a drop of it with you in a bottle and keep it in your pocket. Your wife will be on the last horse and snatch her,' said she.

He did as she asked him and he was there.

'Snatch her and pull her down,' said she.

'It's hard to do it,' said he, 'but I'll try it,' said he.

He did, and he caught her (and he pulled her down off the horse and brought her home).

And she was at Mass the following Sunday, and we all saw her at Mass. But she was very quiet (from then on) – I suppose she wasn't allowed to give any information. She lived to be a good age. She would speak to anyone who spoke to her, you know, but she had no chit-chat as another woman would. It was inside in Puleen in Ardgroom that she lived.

*Bewitching [the evil eye]*

There weren't many of those around with years – they were there long ago no doubt – anyone there was any doubt about that he would put the evil eye on that person: for example if I were to come in now, as I did a while ago, and that you would be inside and that we would be talking. Right. I would say to you: 'How are you?'

'*Erú*, I'm not good at all: I don't be too well at times' (you would say).

If you had any complaint then, whether it would be the mother or the woman of the house, she would say (maybe): 'You didn't have any complaint until that man came in a while ago. Maybe it's the way he bewitched you.'

Bewitching comes from begrudgery. Right. They would be sent out then, whether it was a son or daughter of hers who would have been bewitched, calling that person who had left the house: whether it was a man or a woman, they would be sent for and be brought in.

I saw it done. He would have to spit on that person, three times … 'in the name of the Father and of the Son and of the Holy Spirit.'

I saw it done in this place since I came here. It was a man, you know, who was fine and fat for himself. And a woman came in …

'Get out with you,' said the woman, when she came in, 'and do something. It won't be long until you can't stir, you are so fat!'

And she didn't say 'God bless you' or anything.

He became sick when the woman went out. His mother said to him to get up and go out and do something.

'I'm not able,' said he.

'Why won't you do something?' said she. 'What's wrong with you?'

'I don't know,' said he. 'I can't do anything since Peig Crowley came in.' She was sent for then no doubt: they weren't far from one another (the two houses), and the woman – Peig Crowley – came in.

'I bewitched you?' said she.

Right. She came down – he was stretched on the seat – and she spat on him three times, and nobody heard her saying any prayer.

'Oh wisha, long bewitching on you!' said she. He was not well for a week, and his mother went calling her again and she did not come at all.

Well, I heard a poor woman saying, one time, that you could not do it – bewitching – to any man or woman who would have lived for any length of time, but that you could do it to a child who would be good-looking. That is the result of not being baptised properly, a holy man said – it wasn't a priest who said it at all – that the evil eye was the result of not being baptised properly. The people who stood for him (for the person with the evil eye) did not say the prayers properly. It wouldn't be a good thing for them to look at your child or your cow or your little calf, he said. It's in them unknown to themselves.


THINGS WITH PROPERTIES OF MAGIC AND LUCK

*1. The luck of the smoke*

They didn't like to see any smoke before sunrise – that is on May Morning. There was a woman in Inward Ardgroom, and whatever she ever heard before that, she had it.[4] She got up on May Morning, early in the morning before sunrise: she didn't make any fire herself on that occasion.

When she came out she didn't see any smoke anywhere only smoke she saw to the north in Kerry – to the west of Sherky.[5] She saw smoke there. But she said: 'The luck of that smoke on my butter.'

There was a man walking the road under her, and she was up on a *cnocán*, and when she used to say: 'The luck of that smoke on my butter,' he used say: 'Half of that to me.'

But she didn't see or hear him. Right. The time came when the man came around the following Christmas. And she used to have a lot of butter – firkins. The man who used to bring the firkins to Cork came to her like this one day. He came into the dairy with her – a carter who used to buy the butter from her …

'Haven't you any more butter than that after the year?' (he said).

'I didn't make anything like the amount of butter,' said she, 'that I would have liked to.'

'And what happened to you?' said he.

'I don't know,' said she, 'but I didn't make as much butter as I should have.'

That was the woman who used to say: 'The luck of the smoke on my butter'.

Well, before she died, she told the story to the priest on her deathbed.

'Ah,' said the priest, 'it wasn't right for you at all to get up and say, "the luck of that smoke on my butter".'

But it came to pass that the man said that he sold ten firkins that he had never sold before that – that it was probably someone else's butter he had.

### 2. The angel (i)

Well, the ashes that would be in the fire after May Eve, no grain of them would be put out. They would put it in a pot oven and leave it inside until the next day, because they used to say that the 'Holy Angel' used be in them. They used call the embers, the Holy Angel.

*Tadhg Ó Murchú*: Did you ever hear that there was any cure in the ashes from the fire, or that they had any virtue?

*Peig Minihane*: I never heard that there was any cure in them.

### 3. The angel (ii)

Embers from the fire, they used call them the Angel. They used to say that if you walked Ireland and had a little bit of the Angel in your pocket, that no spirit would come near you. I saw that being done often – [by] people who would be going out late at night. It was a woman I heard saying it, one night when we were up there at the foot of the mountain at a wake, and she was storytelling – entertaining the people at the wake. But she told this story about the salt – how it got its taste – but I didn't bring it with me.[6]

### 4. Spitting on money

Oh, I saw that being done to a hundred things besides the fishing rod.[7] When they used get the money they used spit on it. And there used be other people who wouldn't like to sell anything on Monday: they wouldn't like to let the money go on Monday.

### 5. The four-leafed shamrock

I had a brother west in Kilcatherine, God's blessing on his soul: he is dead for a long time: he died in America. He got it, wisha, the four-leafed shamrock. He knew well what he had, and he put it firmly tied into his trouser pocket – the shamrock. He had it a couple of months, and I suppose the trousers were in need of the needle to put a piece on them – to mend them – and he didn't think of the shamrock – he didn't think of the shamrock being in his pocket. He threw them to his mother at night to put the piece on them, they were torn from the spade – I remember it well and I a little one. When she went putting a piece on the trousers, she put a hand in the pocket, searching for buttons to put them in the trousers, and she came across the shamrock – she didn't see it at all – she pulled out everything that was in the pocket searching (for the buttons). He told her in the morning to throw them up on the loft to him.

He said nothing until he missed the shamrock. There wasn't one bit of the house that he didn't search with his two hands to see if he could find it, but he didn't.

You see, it was always said, in the place where a foal would be born, that the shamrock was growing there. And it was true for them: it's there that he found it. It was after that that he told (where he found it) when it was gone from him – in the field near the house. The person who would have it, there was no danger that if he was to lose a hundred pounds but that he would find it (again); even so, he was not permitted to give any information: you couldn't show it to anyone or tell anyone that you had it.

### 6. Stale urine [Maothachán]

Upon my word that I saw a woman doing it – I slept in the same bed as her – blessing herself with it (with the stale urine).

*1. A prohibition against raking the ashes at night*
I never threw any ashes down on my fire (raked up its ashes before going to bed), but I used put a few sods under the embers.

*2. A prohibition against sleeping on the rack*
*Tadhg Ó Murchú*: Did you ever hear that it was forbidden to sleep on the rack in the kitchen at night?
*Peig Minihane*: I did, and some person said then that the poor people (wanderers) had no place only the rack.

But Máire Ní Mhurchú told them then to make a bed for the poor person on the floor and to leave the rack to them (the people from the other world).

*3. A prohibition against a lone person*
It is forbidden for a lone person to go calling the priest to a sick person at night, or looking for a midwife, without someone else being with them.

*4. The feet water*
The family who would wash their feet in the water on their way to bed – the 'feet water' they used to call it – that should be thrown out at night (and) if any (evil) thing came outside it couldn't come in. Before going to bed at all they used hear murmuring outside the door (calling for) the feet water, to let them in. And one night the woman of the house was going to bed …

'Mistress,' said the talk outside the door, 'don't throw out the feet water.'

'I have it thrown out,' she said.

The feet water spoke then:

'I'm thrown out here under your feet,' said the feet water to the voice outside.

But never again did she throw out the feet water – she left it inside.

*5. Having the clean water in at night*
Máire Ní Mhurchú, God's blessing on her soul, said that the clean water should be in for the night, and a basin or some vessel

beside it, and to stock up the house (the kitchen) no doubt. I used to do that always.

1 This Irish expression probably refers to Máire Ní Mhurchú's contact with the 'good people' or fairies but is difficult to translate directly.
2 Urine.
3 She is referring here to the man who did not bring his spade home [No. 6, p. 29].
4 Remembered it.
5 Sherky Island [Oileán Seircí] on the Kerry side of the Kenmare River.
6 Remember it.
7 The bait you would throw out to the fish – Tadhg Ó Murchú.

# THE MYTHOLOGICAL TRADITION

*1. A boy who heard the fairy music at night*
I had a brother in Kilcatherine and he wasn't married – he was a young boy. I will start at the beginning for you:

There was a school mistress in Kilcatherine, in the school that is in Kilcatherine at present, and she was staying in the house of a poor woman who had no one but herself: she was lodging with her.

They had company every night then, and they used have dancing and music – puss music – when the mistress was there. They used be there late then, and he [my brother] used to stay late, because he had a liking for the songs and the fun. He took a short cut then (one night) from that house in order to go home, and when he had come some of the way – it wasn't too far – he heard the activity and the music before him. Well, he sat down: there was a ditch, and a step going across the ditch, and he put a leg over the ditch and he sat down listening to the music which was a little away from him, I suppose five or six perches. If he had kept to the path he would have come out just where they were. But he didn't: he took another path around it.

When he came into the house – it was said when you would see the light, anyone who would see anything, that they would fall. His mother was stretched on the seat, falling asleep, you know. It was late I suppose …

'There is a pot of potatoes on the fire for the pigs for the morning,' she said, 'and take them down.'

He didn't say a word, and she sat up and she saw him, and what was he only after fainting.

'Yes,' said she, 'you are out late every night, and you have the result of it now!'

He didn't give her any answer, and she went down to call her husband: she called his father ...

'Get up,' said she. 'There is something wrong with Micheál.'

'What's wrong with him?' he said.

'Oh, whatever is wrong with him,' she said, 'I'm afraid that he is dying.'

'*Dherú*, shush, shush, shush, shush!' said he.

From that night on – and he took a trip to America after that – he wasn't the same boy. And he married, and he went (he died) when it was not expected at all.

There is another world there, and it's no use for us to be denying it either. May God give the best passage to all our souls.

## 2. Fairy music, a match and activity on the mountain

There were two men from this place and they were going to Castletown, and there was no fair at the Bridge (Ardgroom Bridge) at that time. They went off together and they had two beasts each. But they went in the dead of night in order to be south in time for the fair with the dry stock. When they went west from the place where the schoolhouse is now (Ardgroom School) – west from the schoolhouse – they heard the activity, and the rushing about, north of them in the mountain, in a place where there was no house, only the mountain ...

'What's this?' said one of them to the other man. 'What's this music to the north of us?'

'It doesn't matter to you,' said he, 'there is something going on there and we have nothing to do with them and we have no business with them, thanks be to God,' said he.

And they went off and the activity was going on and the match. They saw nothing of them.

It's often I heard old people who used to come here to the old man who was here, and they used to be relating those events.

## 3. Liam Dhonncha and the fairies

There was a boy there west. He was married in Canfie. We used call him Liam Dhonncha. He was coming from a walk at night, and when he came east, there is a cross west there turning down to your left hand side, and there are a couple of houses down there a bit east of the road, and there is a little inlet down there, at the end of the road. When he was coming to the cross, he saw the man standing and walking over and back. When he came to him, he said: 'Good night.'

'Stay there awhile,' said the man, 'I have a job for you.' He stood there. 'I'm here watching you for a while,' said he, 'and I give you my hand and my word that I will put you back in this very spot before the cock crows,' said he.

'Oh, I won't go,' said he. 'It's too late.'

'Oh, my hand and my word to you if you go with me that nothing will happen to you.'

'What do you want me for?' said Liam.

'I will tell you,' said he. 'We are playing a match in Kerry, and we are a man short, and there is a boat with six oars on her,' said he, 'down at the foot of this boreen that we are on now.'

Right. It was no use. He couldn't bring him with him – this was a boy who had no knowledge of matches (but) he was great fun.

'I am afraid,' said the man, 'that it won't go well for you, and if you come with me now,' said he, 'I give you hand and word that I will put you back here again on this spot.'

Right. He didn't go with him, anyway, and he came home, and he told the story to his mother in the morning.

'Oh,' said she, 'it's no wonder that you would meet something. You are out too late.'

And he had five or six of a family. The following night, he spent the night severely ill, and, if he did, he took to the bed sick and the next day he had the priest and the doctor and he was bad. Right. The doctor said – whatever they called him: 'He has brain fever,' said he. The priest said nothing, and his wife asked him if there was anything that would save him.

'Ah,' said the priest, 'it's not right to be out too late.' That's all he said.

A couple of nights after that he was bad, and his mother's brother, he was west at the bridge (Ardgroom Bridge) and he came east to let her get to bed (she was up watching over him). She was fairly old. They went to bed and he stayed up, and from the time that the last of them went to bed the music started behind the back door and he [Liam] started to dance to the music at the end of the bed, keeping time to the music with his two feet on the end of the bed that he was stretched in. The uncle went down to him …

'Is it dancing you are to the music that's behind the door?' (said the uncle). He gave him no answer, and he turned his head in (to the wall) laughing.

'Ha, ha!' said the uncle, 'there's no danger that I'll come here any other night looking after you,' by the way, to frighten him. Right. He – the uncle – told his sister – every word in the morning.

'We'll pull out the fire,' said she, 'and we'll put him under it, and we'll throw him out the back door to them altogether,' said she. He gave a big peal of laughter out of him below.

A week from that night he was being waked, God save us from the likes of it!

### 4. The midwife who was taken into the lios[1]

*Tadhg Ó Murchú*: Used they be paid – the midwives?

*Peig Minihane*: Oh, they used to get a little, you know – a crown or four shillings – a crown (they used get for it) day and night.

*Tadhg Ó Murchú*: I suppose that they had no training like that in nursing, that they had plenty of neck!

*Peig Minihane*: Neck no doubt. And maybe some people couldn't give them anything (any pay).

There was one of them coming from Castletownbere – it's not far away – coming to Ardgroom, herself and another woman – a midwife. They were there coming east from Barrs Bridge – they were east of that, a little – in the evening, and there was a frog jumping before them out on the road, east of the bridge …

'Wisha, God love you, creature' (said the midwife), 'I would help you if I was near you.' She noticed that it had a big litter of young in its belly.

It was the will of the world that she was called after that around nine o'clock in the night, it was said, and she was taken in to where there was a big gathering there, of people – into a *lios*.

When she saw that it was to a *lios* that she was being brought, she would not go in. A woman came to her …

'Well, you promised that you would come,' said she, 'and when you gave your promise,' said she, 'you will have to answer. You will be brought home safe and sound again,' said she.

She came and she had to go into the *lios*. She did her business and she was put back.

A woman came to her when she had her business done …

'You will get plenty money now,' she said, 'and don't take one penny of it. You will be put out again and, whatever you do, don't take any penny from them.'

She was a woman who was a relative of hers who was inside in the *lios* (who gave her the advice) – it was in that *lios* west there in Corrach (at the foot of Canfie) that that happened. Yes, no doubt.

### 5. A cow that was carried off

Was I telling you about the cow that died in Lauragh and was carried off? You know where the schoolhouse is east there in Lauragh? That's the place where the man was living (the man who owned the cow). But the man was working in Dereen – I knew him well – and he only had one cow – a fine grey cow. I knew the cow too, and his wife.

But the cow died, God keep us, on the man, and he had a young family, and the poor woman was crying and lamenting after the cow – she was as good as two cows. Well, there was a man – he came to her – who used often be in the company of the 'good people': he was from the Glen east, from Glentrasna, and he was advising the woman not to be crying after her …

'However much you needed the cow,' he said, 'they needed her as much in the place where she went, and don't be crying any more.' Well, the night was there then … 'And shame on ye,' he said, 'why did ye skin her? Would you like to see your cow now?' said he.

'Wisha, I would,' said she.

'Well, come with me and you will see your cow,' said he.

She went off with him, and there was a big *lios* a bit up from her, in Lauragh, and he brought her up to the *lios*. Well, she saw her cow standing like any cow, with no skin on her, and she didn't cry a tear after that then, and the man had meal and flour and a big shop after that then, and he got on fine, and he didn't have anything only his day's pay before that from the Marcus (The Marquis O'Landsdowne).

## 6. A sick man seen out riding

*Tadhg Ó Murchú*: And did the old people not say also that people sick in bed used be seen outside?
*Peig Minihane*: It's often I heard it, that they used be seen outside no doubt.

I had a brother west in Kilcatherine and he was seen out riding on his horse. He was sick, and well sick too, and the postman came here to me with a letter – I was married here at that time – but it wasn't a letter from him but from America. But the postman said to me that my brother was given up for dead by priest and doctor.

Right. I went west (to see him) and when I went west, I went into the post office anyway, and the postwoman – she is dead for a long time, God give her grace – and she heard everything that I had heard here [and] that convinced me (that my brother was given up for dead).

'Take it easy,' said she. 'That's a lie,' she said. 'There is a man from Inches,' she said, 'working here on the road, and I asked him if he heard anything about Micheál Minihane.'

'Before I left Inches, Micheál Minihane passed me by on the road on horseback, and I tell you that he was moving,' he said. 'I had to move in to the side of the road from him.' Right. He said to her that it was a lie she had been told; that he met him himself and he on his horse. 'But he is not sick anyway,' he said.

Right. I headed off and I went to Kilcatherine, and he was sick in the bed before me and well sick, and the doctor was in the room with him – from Castletownbere. A neighbour man came in and he stayed up in the kitchen until the doctor came up from the room and he went down to see him then …

'I was to Eyeries today, Mike,' he said, 'and you met me and where were you going?'

He turned in to the wall and laughed: 'And you had no fear that the horse would knock you.'

But his wife said then: 'Where did you meet him Paddy?' The man was Paddy Murphy.

'In Ballycrovane,' said he, 'and he flying through the air wherever he was going – it was coming home he was.'

Right …

'Get up out of that,' said Murphy. 'It's play-acting you are,' said he. 'You met me on the road all right and I spoke to you, and you answered me but I did not understand you,' said he.

'Did you see Paddy Murphy yesterday?' said she (his wife). That was the next day after I being west, and she was trying to get him out of the bed, by the way.

He said that he did see him: 'I did,' said he.

'Where did you see him?' said she.

'It was in Ballycrovane I met him,' said he.

'Where were you going?' said she. 'You never left this house yesterday.

'Ah, walking,' said he.

The next morning then, she went off at dawn, when the cock crew, looking for the boundary water for him. She was trying to bring the eldest boy – he was eighteen years old – with her for company, and he (the sick man) said to her, whatever she did, not to bring him with her – I suppose he knew that he himself was gone and that that was no small thing.

'I will not frighten you,' said he.

Well she went to the place where the boundary water was. While she was taking the water – she had the bottle under the water – she heard the laughing, and the laughing, and the laughing to the south of her – the activity and the laughing, as if they were dancing, she said – the gathering!

She fled with the drop of water, and upon my word, nothing saved him. He went, and he was gone long before he went, because others saw him, because something happened to him on his way home from walking at night.

They are there too, whatever kind they are (the fairies). We refuse to believe in them.


Pookas and Spirits

*1. A boy who was led astray on New Year's Eve*
I had a boy here and he was out on New Year's Eve. Well, he was

out late, and late, and I couldn't understand what was keeping him, because he wasn't a rake at all, but he had a voice that would wake the dead, it was so beautiful.

I was in and out all night until it was, I suppose, twelve o'clock, and he wasn't coming.

No matter what road he took the dog would follow him, anyway, before that. I was sitting on a chair or a seat by the fire, after being outside. I came in, and the dog came in and it came in beside me and started to 'hu, hu, hu, hu' beside me, as it looked at me. Right. It went down the floor, the dog, and it went as far as the threshold, and it looked in, whining.

'Well now boy, you know where he is,' I said.

It went off and I followed it and it took me to the place where he was, and where was he only stretched in a dyke and the water over him. And the first thing I did was to catch his collar to see if it was closed, and it wasn't. It was open on him. He was able to breathe: I suppose he was in need of it. Right. I was debating with him then ...

'Shame on you,' said I, 'what happened to you?' said I.

'Oh mother, *a chroí*,' he said, 'forgive me for that. It's how I was led astray and I didn't know where I was. Well, as long as I live on this earth you won't see me like that. Whatever put me astray, I was put astray,' said he.

Well, I stayed there with him for a while until he came to, and we walked up the scout which is east there until we came to the house, and upon my word, he didn't make any delay until he made his way to the bed – in the way that he wouldn't take a drink or a bite. Right.

The next day he said this much: 'Were you down to the road,' he said, 'since nightfall? Well,' he said, 'there was some woman there: there was a woman standing for a long time outside me on the road,' said he, 'and I knew it wasn't you because she had a cloak on her,' said he.

And there was a woman east there living on the south side of the road and she used come here every holiday night, and when she came in – this was before this happened ...

'As I was on my way here now,' said she, 'along the road, I saw a woman with a cloak on her and her back to the ditch,' said she, 'and I didn't recognise her at all,' said she. 'I spoke,' said she 'but I wasn't answered.' She was after coming in here. Well, she said then: 'It wasn't any woman of this world who was there.' It was later that my son went that way. 'And I spoke to her twice,' said she, 'and she didn't answer me, and she had a cloak on her,' said she, 'and she had a white bonnet on her head.'

It was early in the night. Well, the following day she took a short cut on her way to the house: she didn't take the road at all. Well, after that, the boys were going to the bridge west, on New Year's Eve, I think, and in the same place that she saw the woman there was a blaze of fire there – in the same spot. And in the morning when he got up – one of the boys who was there – he went west to see if the mark of the fire was there, but it wasn't.

## 2. *A girl who was lifted into the air*
There was a woman west there in Kilcatherine, and I suppose it isn't more than forty years ago, and she had two little girls, around fourteen and fifteen. She sent them herding the cows on a Sunday evening. She said to herself (then) that they were long enough there – the cows – and that she would call them (the two girls) to turn them out and bring them home: there was a little bit of the field tilled. She went out on the ditch, a little way from the house, in a place where she had a good view of the girls who were herding the cows and she called on them to drive out the cows. And while she was doing that she saw one of them rising from the ground and going up in the air as far as she could see:

'Great God,' she said, and she became dazzled, she said. Upon my word I heard her say it, the mother.

Right. She came in and she told her story inside: there was an old woman in the house. *Erú*, they said that she was raving – how could she rise into the air?

'Oh she did,' she said.

'And did she come down?' they said.

'If she did, I didn't see her,' she said.

She did come down too, and if she did, upon my word dear, she was there, and when she came home she was very upset.

'Where were you going?' her mother said. 'I saw you rising up in the air,' she said. 'Where were you going?'

But she was sick the next day. But they asked the other little girl who was with her if she saw her going up in the air, and she said that she didn't. But upon my word she went. Wherever she was going she went to eternity.

*Tadhg Ó Murchú*: She died?

*Peig Minihane*: Oh she did. She became sick, and there was only a week between that day and the day she died. No doubt that was all there was.

You wouldn't hear any of that now, thanks be to God – in the middle of the day! That's a sister of hers there now with JD. The girl who was with her was left, she wasn't interfered with – only the sister.

## 3. *The Pooka of Darkness*

There used be another type going around – that used to have a light – that they used to call the Pooka of Darkness. He used to have a light, and he would put you astray, he used to have such a blaze of light. Long, long ago (he used be there).

## 4. *The Blackberry Pooka*[2]

There used be some other kind there that they used to call Jackie (and) the Blackberry Pooka. On St Michael's Night (he used to be going around) and from then on nobody would taste them (the blackberries). He used to visit them, and I declare to the world that they used to turn a dark grey colour from St Michael's Night on.

## 5. *A light at night*

I had two boys here. Well, they weren't very old: one of them was eighteen years, and the other was fifteen years.

There was a man up here – a man of the Sheehan family – longside us: he was not very far from us at all, and he told the two of them to go up the following night – that was Thursday night – threshing oats. They used to thresh it inside in the house at that time, certain people. And they went. They took a short cut down, across: they didn't go the road at all and they had the road from the door. And as they came together, after ten o'clock – coming home – half-way between this house and that house east, a blaze of light came between them, and one of them saw it and the other one didn't see it at all.

'Do you see the light?' said he.

'I don't,' he said. 'Where is it?'

'Don't you see it there?' he said.

'I don't see it at all,' he said.

People a long time ago used to say that no one saw anything from the other world, only the person who would stand for you and not say the prayers properly (the result of improper baptism).

SUPERNATURAL ANIMALS

### 1. The black hound and the priest

There was a priest who was west there in the little village west (Eyeries), and two men went calling him at night to anoint the old man – I suppose it was the dead of night. The (priest's) little mare was going fast and they couldn't keep up with him at all (the two men); it was the father (of one of them) who was dying. But he was dead before them when the priest came: it was a colic that he got. But the priest said to them: 'Will ye go with me now?' he said.

They said that they would, for a while.

'Oh, ye will have to leave me west into the house where ye found me,' said he. They saw nothing, but he announced on the altar the following Sunday what happened to him. He said that never again would he go annointing anyone in the dead of night. It was a black hound, he said, that he met, and it was across, over and back under the belly of the horse.

And notice how he wouldn't go west home again without the two men accompanying him!

He was afraid, I suppose, after the terror he had gone through. He took out a bottle of holy water and shook it on them (on the two men, when they left him west).[3]

### 2. The cows from the other world

There was a man east there in Eisc a' Dobhair, God's blessing on his soul, and he used be out at night walking, you know – Michael Sheehan. As he was coming home at night, he saw a man with two cows – a colour that nobody ever saw before (on any cow) – speckled – and he herding them, and turning them hither and thither in the field. He stopped and examined them well.

The next morning then, he went into the mountain after sheep or cows – this man. He saw the same two cows in the mountain, in a mountain hollow, in a smooth level place, and he said that he recognised them – the two cows. Well, he was looking at them for a while. Right then. He turned from them and he recognised them, that they were the two cows he saw the night before. Right. He didn't put in or out on them, and he went his way and went home.

Well, there was a neighbour man in the mountain the next day after cows or sheep and he saw the two cows and he had no idea that the other man had seen them the day before. He saw the two cows and he sat on a *cnocán* above them – the man – the next day.

He didn't think of anything and he went down looking at the two cows, and he never saw any two cows before of that colour – white and speckled, and every colour that he never saw before.

The next night he fell sick and he told his story and everyone said that he shouldn't have gone after them at all when he had never seen them before – the two strange cows.

Right. He came home and fell badly sick, and sick and sick. Right. There was a man in Kilcatherine who used be looking after the sick people, and they used to say that he had special knowledge, but he hadn't. But they sent for him and he came and went up – it was up in Cuhig that the sick man was. But this man came and he examined him.

'You are sicker than you think,' he said.

'Oh, I'm not sick at all,' he said, 'but I'm weak.'

'Oh, you are sicker than you think,' he said. His wife and family were there, in the house, and his mother: she was heading for eighty, I'm sure.

The man came up from the room and the mother spoke: 'What do you think of him?' his mother said.

'Whatever way he is, let someone go for the priest.'

His mother beat her two palms.

'*Erú*, maybe it's a drop he is after drinking!'

'I haven't drunk any drop that would put me astray,' he said.

There was a neighbour man inside and his mother said to him – the mother of the sick man who was in the bed – when he ordered the priest, you know: '*Erú*, he's a fool of a man!' she said, 'and don't take any notice of him, calling for the priest.'

'I'm not calling for him at all,' said the man in the bed, 'nor have I any need for him.'

'Very well,' said the man (from Kilcatherine). 'Do what ye like! Let ye bring the priest to the man in the bed: he will be with his Saviour by morning,' he said.

*Erú*, his wife and mother went abusing him, and he went out the door from them.

'Do what ye like!' said he.

'Well,' said the man in the bed, 'I have no need for a priest tonight anyway.'

'And what will we do if anything happens to you?' said his mother, 'and if you like we will call the priest for you.'

Well, they went calling the priest, two boys and this man, and the priest was only down on the road when he drew his [last] breath. They were cursing him (at first – the man from Kilcatherine), and they had plenty blessings for him later, no doubt.


SUPERNATURAL PLACES

*1. A closed door on a lios*

There is a *lios* in Corrach. It was said – and it was often said – that there was an iron door in there and that you could not go past that, and that it was inside there that the Norsemen had the gold, when they were living there.

Some wise man who went the road said that they asked his advice, and he said: 'Well,' said he, 'you will do all right, but one of you will die if you go after it.'

They backed out then: they didn't go there at all, because they didn't know whose lot it would fall to.

## 2. Lios na gCat [the Lios of the Cats]

There is a *lios* west, on the south side of the old road (to Eyeries) – *Lios na gCat* [the *Lios* of the Cats]. It used be full of wild cats long ago – cats that used go around the district and become troublesome.

They used to bury children there too, who were not baptised – who were not baptised in time. They used to.

## 3. Máire Eoghain and the Comhla Bhreac (Speckled Door)[4] of Béal na Leapa

There was another woman from Canfie, to this side (east) of the village (Ardgroom Village): she used be in their company (the fairies).

But one day herself and the husband and two or three others were coming from Castletown, on a fair day in the evening. Máire Eoghain was her name. When they were in Béal na Leapa … there is a road coming from the north-east, from Kilmackowen, at the cross here, and the King's road going below it west – there are four roads leaving one cross. And when you would be going to Castletown, on your left hand side, there is a cliff there that is a mile high. Well, herself and her husband and three other women were coming from Castletown and two men came out of the quagmire of water – the cliff is called the *Comhla Bhreac*. Some kind of sounds used be heard there at night. Two men came out before them on the road and one of the men put his hand on the shoulder of the Canfie woman and he said to her: 'Come out of the cart,' he said, 'there is business here for you for a while,' said he. The man stopped the horse and she got down. 'Follow me now,' said he.

'*Erú*, the place is too wet,' said she.

'It doesn't matter to you,' said he, 'but follow me or you will be sorry' (she followed).

But she said that there was a gathering of people inside in the cliff: it opened up (when they came to it). But she didn't tell anyone why they brought her there. But a man came out then …

'Let ye wait there now,' said he, 'and she will be out to ye in a minute.'

She was brought out again as far as the cart.

### 4. The old Eyeries road

I didn't hear anything since I came to Ardgroom – anything worth mentioning – but anyone who would go the old road … a lot used be seen on the old road.

They say that anyone who goes the old road now – we avoid it – anything that is seen or heard, that it is on the old road that it is seen, but nothing is seen on the new road.


## THE HAG OF BEARA

### The Hag of Beara and the crab

The Hag went down one day, and when she was at her ease, she went down shore gathering, and she put her hand in under a flat stone that was on the strand – some heavy flat stone – looking for little fish, and what did the crab do only catch her tightly by the finger, and she was there then and every screech out of her.

A man came to her, one of the neighbours, to see what was making her shout.

'What is wrong with you,' said the man, 'that you are shouting?'

'I went down to the strand,' she said, 'and I put my hand under a flat stone looking for little fish, and the crab caught me by the finger.'

'Oh, show it to me,' said the man. 'Have you got the crab?'

'Oh, I have,' said she. 'It's a bad man who isn't better than nothing.'

'May yourself and itself croak!' said the man, 'if that's your story.'

'Oh, I'll keep it, my bright leggy crab.'

'*Erú*, may it croak!' said the man. 'Throw it into the fire!'

'Oh, I won't,' said she, 'my bright leggy crab. It's a bad man who's not better than nothing.'

The man left her then. A young girl came to her then that evening, where she was, in the strand: she didn't go in (to her) at all.

'Come out to me please,' said the girl. 'I would like to talk to you,' said she.

'Be off with you from here. Mind your own business!' said the Hag.

'Oh, I won't,' said she, pulling out her magic wand, and drawing three pulls – three blows – of the magic wand on her, and she made a stone of her. This man (who went to save her), he was somewhere in the east of the strand and he had a view west over the strand.

1 Enclosed ground of ancient dwelling-house, ringfort – thought to be fairy dwelling place.
2 'See over there the pooka shitting on the blackberries on St Michael's Day' – Tadhg Ó Murchú.
3 It is my confident opinion that the two men that this happened to were Diarmaid Ó Sé, Fán Shliabh and his wife's brother – Tadhg Ó Murchú.
4 Speckled Door – entrance to fairy dwelling-place.

# POPULAR ORAL LITERATURE

*1. Neil na gCopóg [Nell of the Docks] – storyteller*
Well, there was a woman there in Inward Ardgroom, and she was called *Neil na gCopóg* [Nell of the Docks] and there was no story that was ever composed that she did not have. I never saw her with my own eyes, nor did I see her in any way that she would come across me, but there used be great demand for her in wake houses for storytelling. They couldn't go to a wake house at all if she wasn't there.

*2. Tadhg na Féithe [Tadhg of Fay], Daniel O'Sullivan and other storytellers*
Oh, they had stories all right, and they used be telling them. But if the young people looked after the stories, there would be stories after them.

There was one man there – they used to call him *Tadhg na Féithe* [Tadhg of Fay] – Tadhg Rohane (Mac Carthy) was his name – as good a storyteller as I ever heard – he was known to everyone: 'You are as good as *Tadhg na Féithe*,' (they used to say), 'as good as *Tadhg na Féithe*' – anyone who would be a good talker.
*Tadhg Ó Murchú*: Did you ever hear him telling stories?
*Peig Minihane*: Oh, I didn't – he was too far from me – but he had the road from when he used leave the door, and even if the day was snowing he would make his way to Mass. Oh, he had stories without any doubt.
*Tadhg Ó Murchú*: Used he be any night in your house?
*Peig Minihane*: He used not, but a neighbour used be every night of the year with us, and if we looked after him – but we didn't, we used to be at the books – we would have stories.

My husband's father was here, and he was as good a story-teller as I ever heard – he was Daniel O'Sullivan. He is dead for

a good while no doubt, in his grave, God's blessing on his soul
– for nearly fifty years. I (myself) am eighty-eight years now – I
won't hide my age – and I was twenty-one when I came here.
When people are getting on in years, too old, they don't keep account of these stories at all – their minds become bothered. They
become scattered no doubt – they do, dear.

### 3. Ghost stories gone from the world now

I never saw a spirit or a pooka, thanks be to God, since the day
that any sense came into my head. I never saw anything, but I
heard [things]. I didn't ever tell it, and I won't tell it now, because
you wouldn't keep it to yourself.[1] The people who are growing
up now, they wouldn't listen to anything like that; and they used
to see them long ago, and they used to come talking to them
(people from the other world).


## Poets

### 1. Seán a' Bháin Mhóir [Seán of Bán Mór] – poet

He was east there in Lauragh and he married into a farm south
in Adrigole. Oh, he was an important poet, but I don't have any
of his songs.

### 2. A girl who had the gift of poetry

There was a man at the butt of a hill around Eyeries and he was
going for the cows in the evening to bring them home, and he
met a wanderer, and he asked the cowman would he put him up
until morning. He said that he would …

'Go up now to the house,' said he, 'because I am going for
the cows. That's my house up there.'

Right. During the night he asked the man (of the house) if
there was any poet around the place who had any poetry.

'There's not,' said the man of the house, 'but there's one girl
who is deadly at rhymes.'

'I would like to see her,' said the wanderer – he was a poet.

'You won't be able to see her until tomorrow,' he said.

'Very well,' he said.

'There's a girl here west of us,' said he (the man of the house), 'and she has two brothers and her father. They will be gathering seaweed down on the strand tomorrow and she will bring the dinner to them, and you will have a trial of her then.'

'Ah *mo léir*,' said the poet, 'and how will I know her, or what road she will take?'

'I will go with you,' said he. 'She will be going down with the dinner when the tide is coming.'

Right. (The next day) they went off.

'*Dherú*, where would she get poetry,' said the wanderer, 'at the butt of a hill here?'

'Don't mind that,' said the man. 'Maybe she has poetry too. Speak to her,' said he, 'when she meets you.'

Right. She came upon them. And it wasn't long until they saw the boat coming in a little away from them, and it wasn't long until they saw the girl coming with a covered basket and potatoes and fish in the basket. Right. When she came down ...

'Oh trotting wench, stay quiet 'til I make a verse for you,' said he.

'Oh,' said she, 'the tide is coming, the men fasting, and it's gone past their time.'

'Oh,' said he, 'it's no lie but she is a poet' – when she gave him his answer.


### 3. Seán The Boy

*Tadhg Ó Murchú*: Did you ever hear tell of Seán The Boy, a poet who lived here in Beara somewhere?[2] He went over to America and he washed his shirt one day, and he hung it on a tree to dry it, and a bull came and ate the shirt on him. He composed a song about the bull and the shirt then.

*Peig Minihane*: I did indeed, and I had the song, but I can't remember it now. But he said anyway:

Oh bull without humanity, a hundred sorrows on you and may you go blind,
And a cloud from the sky on you that will desert you in a bog or a hole:
You had no need in the world, you had grass to eat everywhere,
That you had to come eating my shirt on a sunny day and it hanging from a tree.

I sweated in drops after hanging it on a tree,
(If there was a woman in Ireland beside me who would wash it in
time).

*1. Curly Creepy – an old singer*
There was a man there in Castletown, long ago, who was called
Curly Creepy, and he had two crutches and a chair that he used
to sit on, and he used to be singing the ballads. Oh, he could sing
them sweetly no doubt.

All he had was a little cabin above the street, and he used
have a handbasket, selling apples and he made money.

Right. He was eighty-eight when he died, and there was no
one belonging to him around. And he had a crutch and a walking stick. And when he got old, anyway, he was in bed, and they
were trying to put him in hospital and he wouldn't go there – he
said that he had enough money to have himself looked after [at
home] in bed. Right. When he died, anyway, I suppose they were
searching, and all around him was searched and he had £150, and
the old men used to say: 'Oh great powerful God, how did he
make it?'

He didn't ever make it (I suppose) but got it in a hole in the
ground!

*2. A song in Irish – Cois na Leamhna (air – Moladh na nGleann)*

i
*Cois na Leamhna mar a ngnáthaíonn ba caoire agus gamhna,*
*Caise bog uachtair agus mórchuid den leamhnacht;*
*Eorna throm ina shlaoda ann agus féar glas go glúinibh*
*Agus ceol binn breá ag éanaibh gach aon mhaidean drúchta.*

ii
*Níl cuíora maidean dhrúchta ann gan cúpla aici ag léimrigh*
*Ná bó maidean shamhraidh gan gamhain lena taobh deas;*
*Níl neath óg na seanda gan foghlaim is béasa ann*
*Ná abhlóird gan úlla air ná cárthann gan caorthaibh.*

111

*Is mó ní breá aerach ar an dtaobh so 'Dhrom Eanna,*
*An coinín mhear éadtrom ag léimrigh sa ghainnimh;*
*Úlla cúmhra i ngáirdíní mar a ngnáithíd siad aspail,*
*Agus tiarnaí na dútha ag siúl ann gach maidin.*

I heard a boy singing it (that song) at the Pattern (the Pattern of Loch a' Coinleáin) – a boy from south in the Ranties[3] – singing it inside in a cabin. Oh, I suppose it is around thirty years ago since I heard it. Oh my bitter sorrow, but he had a voice no doubt! He had a glass of drink in his hand and he stood up and sang the song. He was a nice chatty boy.

*3. A fragment of a song from Iveragh*
There was a man there from Iveragh (at the Pattern) – oh *mo léir*, and he had songs! And he had a little wife and she wasn't that height, and he was a fine big man. But he had a song that he used to sing:

> West in Iveragh I was born a child.
> It's there that the potato used be,
> The sturgeon high on the wave,
> And fish going onto the green fields.

BLESSINGS, WISHES AND A LITTLE VERSE

1. 'May you grow old with your family!'
2. 'Good health to you and honest health.'
3. 'May you be in comfort in a year's time and may God prevent any disease from coming amongst us.'
4. 'May God of Glory grant you my prayers – may they come in your direction.'
5. 'May God preserve you and your people from any trouble or disease from today to a year from today.'
6. 'May God preserve us from harmful tobacco.' That's what the old people used to say.
7. 'Oh, Kilcatherine God help us!' (an old saying).

8. 'He has a woman west in Gortahig,
   And a woman in Oileán na gCaerach,
   A woman in the Height of Boffickel,
   And a woman in Droinn na mBéilleac.'

---

1 It was to her son's daughter that she said this. She was urging her to tell me the story, but
  she wouldn't, for fear that the girl would tell on her! – Tadhg Ó Murchú.
2 That was all she knew about Seán. She did not know his surname – Tadhg Ó Murchú.
3 In the Adrigole district, Co. Cork.

# POPULAR PASTIMES

## DANCING

*Tadhg Ó Murchú*: Do you remember the dancing masters who used to be going around teaching dancing?

*Peig Minihane*: Dancing no doubt, wisha. There were two dancing schools in Kilcatherine for two months, no doubt – a dancing master and a piper – Hanley the Piper. There was a famine before that. Well, I don't remember it – I wasn't born at all in the Year of Want or for a long time after.

They were strangers no doubt (the dancing masters). The two of them were together there. The scholars used bring one of them with them every night. They came again after that, after three or four years, and there was a dancing school west there in Canfie.

When I came here to Gurteen from Kilcatherine, there was a dancing school west here in Canfie, in Michael Murphy's shed. Kennedy was the dancing master.

*Tadhg Ó Murchú*: What were the names of the two other masters?

*Peig Minihane*: Oh, I couldn't tell you that, but they were strangers. They were a while there north in Inward Ardgroom – they were there for five or six weeks with a man of the Leahy family who was there.

*Tadhg Ó Murchú*: Used you yourself be learning the dancing?

*Peig Minihane*: Ah, I was at my own school, and I couldn't get permission to go into it except on the benefit night – I couldn't get near it, and I was a better dancer after that than my two sisters who were there. When I used be herding the cows I used be doing the dancing.

*Tadhg Ó Murchú*: I suppose you picked it up from the sisters.

*Peig Minihane*: Erú yes – from the neighbours' girls. And when the day used be good they used be out in the field, in any place where the field would be near them, because the shed used be very small for them all (those learning the dancing).

They used give a shilling a week to the master. One at a time (he used be) teaching them, with a grip on the legs of some of them. They used be describing it like this, a night that there used be drops of sweat, they said, dripping from him – because of some of them who couldn't dance.

The master used have a benefit night when the term was over. They would all be there no doubt – a large gathering. It wasn't inside that they used have that at all but outside, because a half or a third of them wouldn't get room inside. A Benefit Dance they used call it. That was for the dancing master.

Oh, Hanley the Piper was a sweet musician – the dancing master had a violin. He used to help him (the dancing master) any night that he would have any music.

# THE HISTORICAL TRADITION

'Daniel O'Connell, do you understand Irish?'

'I understand well, oh girl from Ireland, and what danger am I in?'

(There was a girl) and she was brushing and cleaning and fussing around the house for herself.

'There's too much salt in that porridge next to you, and don't chance it.'

'Ding, dang, dedaro,' from her then, in case she would be found out.

There were four in the house, and they gave him a dinner invitation (i.e., Daniel O'Connell) – and it was night-time – to come so that they could have a night's drinking, by the way. Right. When whatever was in the glasses (was divided among them), the four who were there, and Daniel O'Connell was the fifth, everyone was given his own glass, and the glass that contained the cider (i.e. the poison) was put before him. There were candles lighting at the head of the table and they all sat down. He – Daniel O'Connell – said then, before they tasted anything:

'I never drank any drink like this, but I drank a shared drink,' said he, 'often, but that I would take off my hat first,' taking hold of his hat. And there were three or four candles lighting on the *crann crithir* (i.e., the candlestick) – that was the name for the holder that the light was on. The *crann crithir*[2] turned over and the light was quenched.

'Oh Powerful God,' he said, 'look what I've done!'

And before it was lit again, Daniel changed the glasses – he took the landlord's one and pushed his own one to the landlord.

'Right, we will drink our drink anyway,' said one of the men.

They all drank their drinks and after a short time Daniel

O'Connell arose and went out and the man of the house followed him.

He went off and he didn't stop three minutes outside – he headed off – and when they didn't come in quickly, the two of them, they went out to see what was keeping them outside – the man of the house and Daniel O' Connell – and Daniel O'Connell was gone and the man of the house was sitting and he couldn't get up from the place where he was.

But some important doctor was called to him, I suppose – he was a big shot I suppose.

'You took poison,' said the doctor, 'and you are finished.'

That was when they found out the truth of the story.

Well, he [Daniel O'Connell] found her anyway – the girl – whatever messenger he sent to her: he would like to see the girl.

And he made a rich woman out of the girl as long as she lived, and they said that she lived to a good age.

---

1 The storyteller uses the name Mac Finín Duibh by mistake instead of Daniel O'Connell a number of times in this story.
2 'Crann crithir' is the Irish for the Aspen tree – the term is obviously being used here for a 'candle holder' of some kind.

Photograph taken on the day Margaret O'Sullivan,
daughter of Roger O'Sullivan and Margaret Crowley (Peig's best friend),
left Barra Coille to return to America in 1936

**Back row (from left): 1** *Patie Crowley, Barra Coille,* **2** *James Healy, Barra Coille
(with cap in hand),* **3** *Dan O'Sullivan (Roger's eldest son),* **4** *Nora O'Sullivan,
Cuhig (the nearest townland to Barra Coille on the Kerry side),* **5** *Margaret O'Sullivan (Roger's daughter – with hat),* **6** *Patsy O'Shea ('Barley'), Gort a' Leasa,* **7** *Noin
Healy, Barra Coille (wife of No. 2),* **8** *Bernard Crowley (brother of No. 1),* **9** *Identity
unknown,* **10** *Margaret Crowley, Barra Coille (Mrs Roger O'Sullivan),* **11** *Jim O'Sullivan, Cuhig (brother of No. 4),* **12** *Peig Minihane,* **13** *Abbey O'Donoghue, Cuhig,*
**14** *Margaret Riney, Ardgroom,* **15** *Roger O'Sullivan, Barra Coille (with hat),* **16** *Mary
O'Sullivan, Cuhig (mother of No. 4 and No. 11, sister of No. 2),* **17** *Bridget O'Shea,
Gort a' Leasa (wife of No. 6),* **18** *Jeremiah O'Sullivan, Barra Coille (Roger's son),* **19**
*Mary O'Sullivan, Cuhig,* **20** *Katie O'Sullivan, Cuhig (sister of No. 4 and No. 11).*

**Middle row (from left): 21** *Rogie O'Sullivan, Barra Coille (Roger's son),* **22**
*Agnes O'Sullivan, Barra Coille (Roger's daughter),* **23** *Child – daughter of Margaret
O'Sullivan,* **24** *Lucy O'Sullivan, Barra Coille (Roger's daughter),* **25** *Lizzy O'Sulli-
van, Barra Coille (Roger's daughter).*

**Front row (from left): 26** *Frances O'Sullivan, Barra Coille (Roger's daughter),* **27**
*John O'Sullivan, Cuhig (brother of No. 4 and No. 11),* **28** *Dora O'Sullivan (with hat
– Roger's daughter),* **29** *Child – daughter of Margaret O'Sullivan,* **30** *Nora
O'Sullivan, Barra Coille (Roger's daughter),* **31** *Lena O'Sullivan, Barra Coille
(Roger's daughter),* **32** *Maggie Crowley (a sister of No. 1 and No. 8).*

# Peig Minihane's
## Family Background and Personality

Around the time of the Famine there were two brothers and a sister of the Minihane (O'Driscoll) family in Doire Mhór, Kilcatherine: Seán Minihane settled down in Carraig, Doire Mhór and married Johanna O'Shea from Kilcatherine; Catherine Minihane, who married Donal [Partolán] Murphy in Doire Ulaidh, Kilcatherine; and Tadhg Minihane, who was called Seana-Thadhg [Old Tadhg], who settled down at home in Doire Mhór West and married Nora Rahilly from Claondoire. These were Peig [Margaret] Minihane's father and mother.

Seana-Thadhg and Nora had nine children: John (January 1851), Daniel (June 1853), Mary (November 1855), Timothy (February 1858) who died young, Timothy (February 1860), Margaret (1861), Patrick (February 1866), Mike (August 1868) who settled down at home in the farm and married Kate Sheehan, The Road, Cathair Caim and Quinlan (June 1871) who lived at home.[1]

Little is known of Peig's youth in Kilcatherine apart from the references she made to it in the material collected from her. But her upbringing in Kilcatherine obviously had a huge influence on her oral repertoire and way of looking at the world, as is evidenced by the number of times that she refers directly to it. Her granddaughter, Noreen Heaney (O'Sullivan), who lived in the same house and knew her intimately for twenty-five years, remembers hearing very little detail from her about her young days in Kilcatherine:

> Yes, she sometimes talked about her young days in Kilcatherine, and of her days in Primary School there. Even though she didn't start school until the age of nine or ten she was an excellent reader and could write and spell very well. She often recited poems which she learned at school, her favourite being 'The Brook' by Tennyson.

She could remember and recite this from beginning to end, and she would always stand up to recite the words of 'Casablanca'. I can still remember her face as if it were yesterday as she started off: 'The boy stood on the burning deck', etc.

She also learned grammar at school, and the parts of speech were learned. She would say: adjective, noun, article, pronoun, verb, adverb, preposition, conjunction and interjection – and always in that order.

She could not read Irish.

I cannot remember much of what she told us of her immediate family. She spoke of her father and the stories he had of Famine days in Ireland. She mentioned an incident of a woman found dead at the side of the road, her mouth being full of grass which presumably she tried to eat before she died of hunger. She had stories of people eating weeds, nettles, etc., but all in all she felt that areas close to the sea having access to fish, shellfish, etc., like Kilcatherine, were not as badly affected by the Famine as more inland areas would have been.

My grandmother seemed to dance a lot in her young days – mostly stepdancing. A dancing master came to Kilcatherine and they learned the various steps. These she never forgot and when we were children she taught us all the basic steps of jigs and reels. She was very light on her feet and she had a great sense of rhythm. She would pull up her long skirt – right up to her knees and dance round the kitchen for us. She would provide her own music for the dance by singing a little tune as she danced. She called this 'puss-music'. If you were awkward or not doing the steps very well she would say: 'You haven't got the ciúta. That meant that you hadn't got that something which makes the difference between a good dancer and a bad dancer.[2]

Here we see Peig as an 'active carrier' of the dancing tradition acquired in her young days in Kilcatherine. However we hear very little of her immediate family. Why did she never speak of her sisters?

I never heard my grandmother speak of her sisters but she often spoke of her brothers. She had one memory of a big brother pulling a shovel down a slope while she sat on the shovel, as a very small child.[3]

When she was twenty-one, a match was made between Peig and

John D. O'Sullivan of Gurteen, Ardgroom. John D.'s father, Daniel O'Sullivan (Breac), first came to Gurteen from a place called Doirín a' tSluaigh in Bunaw in Co. Kerry after the Famine. His wife was Nell O'Sullivan (Suaimhnis) of Colleros. Three of their children, Mary, Peig and John were born in Doirín a' tSluaigh and a fourth, Jerry was born in Gurteen in 1866.[4]

> My grandmother married at the age of twenty-one in 1882, being the same year that Ardgroom National School was built. She had met her husband only once before the wedding. A match was made for them as was customary in those days, even though she did mention having a boyfriend at some stage. She also said that the dancing master liked her a lot!
>
> Her husband was much older than she was. She called him Jack. She walked from Kilcatherine to Gurteen. Her husband's father Daniel lived in Gurteen for many years after she got married. She always spoke of him with great affection. He was a great storyteller and many people used to gather at their house at night to listen to his stories. While the storytelling was going on my grandmother would have a little stool which she placed on top of the long seat, and there she would sit knitting socks from the homespun wool. The reason for placing the stool in this position was to be near the oil lamp which hung high up on the wall.[5]

Peig had thirteen children during her marriage to Jack [John D.], most of whom emigrated to America, never to return: Mary (14 February 1884) went to Salt Lake City, Utah, never returned; Dan (13 November 1885) went to Park City, Utah. He was suffocated in the mines having been only nine months over there; Jeremiah (17 March 1887) also went to Salt Lake City, never returned; John (22 November 1888) died at home, aged sixteen; Patrick (22 January 1891) went to Butte, Montana, never returned; Margaret (24 February 1893) went to Boston, Massachussetts, never returned; Johanna (20 June 1894) went to Boston, Massachussetts, and only came home for a short holiday in 1926; Mike – Mike John D. (16 March 1896) settled down in the farm and married Nora O'Sullivan, daughter of Jimmy O'Sullivan and Mary O'Shea, Droumbeg, Inward Ardgroom; Ellen (13 June 1897) went to Boston, Massachussetts, never returned; Brigid (13 January 1899) died young; Eugene (20 February 1901) went to Boston, Massachussetts, never returned; Peter (29 June 1901) went to Boston, Massachussetts, never returned; Tim (25 November 1903) went to Boston, Massachussetts, never returned.[6]

Apart from the rearing of her many children, Peig worked extremely hard both inside and outside, all through her married life:

> They had some sheep and they carded their own wool. She had a spinning wheel with which she made the thread for knitting. That spinning wheel was still in the house when I was a child. They sold some of the wool in Kenmare which is about twenty miles from Ardgroom. I often heard her talk about the journey to Kenmare, leaving home in the dead of night, pony and cart and load of wool; the long tedious journey; getting out of the cart on the steep hills and pushing the cart to help the pony. They would stop for refreshments at 'Denny Island's'. This was a little wayside inn about four miles from Kenmare, thus named because it faced a little island in the Kenmare estuary. There they would stay until dawn when they would resume their journey to Kenmare for the market. That little building still stands, but it has been closed as a public house for many years.[7]

With her very busy life the birth of her children did not always take place under ideal circumstances:

> My grandfather had a little boat and he and my grandmother used to go out the harbour to collect seaweed to use as a fertiliser for the land. There is a little island (which becomes part of the mainland of Inward Ardgroom at low tide) called Cois. As she and my grandfather were rowing home with a loaded boat of seaweed she got into labour, and so they had to row home as fast as they could. They just about got there on time for her to have the baby. There was a local woman who used to be called to act as midwife. My grandmother was about thirty-five years of age at that time.[8]

However Peig was a woman who was never too wrapped up in her work and cares to be unaware of what was happening in the world around her and she was totally supportive of her family in their Republican involvement:

She often spoke of the time of the 'troubles' and the Black and Tans. She was very involved, as some of her sons were on the run, being Republicans. At that time her husband was very ill (he died in the early 1920s) and she told us about how the Black and Tans came into his bedroom and pushed the guns under his bed lest somebody might be hiding there. The boys were often up on the mountain, and when the Tans left the area she would go out and stand on a high rock and whistle to give the signal that all was clear. Then they would come home. My uncle Eugene and my father Michael were captured and spent some time in Spike Island. My father was a great follower of De Valera, and had a great love for the Irish language. He wore the fáinne [a ring worn on the collar by Irish speakers] all his life, and he taught Irish to some of the prisoners in Spike Island. We have an autograph album which he had in Spike.[9]

And Peig retained her strong political views all her life:

She would be very definite where the voting was concerned, and she knew exactly for whom she wanted to give her number one. The various parties would send out cars to collect the older people from the outlying areas and take them to the school to cast their votes. She would make sure that she travelled only with the party for which she was going to vote.[10]

The gradual loss of so many of her children through death and emigration was borne with great fortitude and strength by Peig, who does not seem to have given in to any form of self pity but managed to steel herself against all her misfortunes and throw herself with great enthusiasm into helping with the rearing of her grandchildren:

My grandmother had thirteen children, eight boys and five girls, all of whom are now dead except for one daughter who I think is still alive and over a hundred years of age, living in the States. One girl, Brigid, died at the age of three from gastro-enteritis. A boy named Johnny died at sixteen, having complained of a headache after being out searching for the wren for St Stephen's Day. He died almost instantly. In all probability it would have been a Christmas Day. All the others, apart from my father, went to America and lived there all their lives. Only one of them, Hannah, ever came home on a visit. She came for a brief holiday in 1926, the year my father got married.

Dan died at a young age in America, but all the others lived to a good old age.

I would say that a day did not pass that my grandmother did not speak of her family in America. She spoke of the sadness of their leaving – going to Castletown where a boat came and took them to Queenstown where they embarked on their voyage to the States. She always got very sad at Christmas time, and when letters and cards arrived (which didn't come in large numbers) the tears would flow freely. But she had a great capacity to regain her cheerfulness and she could be singing within half an hour.

I was twenty-five years of age when my grandmother died in 1957. In fact she died only nine years before my mother passed away. As my father (who was a foreman in the Board of Works) spent much of his time away from home, a few months each year, my mother worked out on the farm quite a lot. So my grandmother was our 'nanny' in every sense of the word. We called her Nain. We all loved her, and when I think of my years in Gurteen, I feel that my grandmother was just as much part of it as were my parents. She would spoil us as children while my mother tried to keep control. She was very generous and everything would be shared. She laughed with us and she cried with us and our little world got her full attention. I think that the great interest which she had in our family helped her to overcome the loneliness and longing which she no doubt had for her own sons and daughters. She had a very outgoing personality and when people visited the house she would more or less take over. Sometimes she would complain about all the work she had to do and at those times she would call herself 'Peig Amadán' ['Peig the fool']. Yet she would never rest even when she was asked to, but she liked the little bit of notice. I remember the day she told me that she was eighty-one years of age. It suddenly struck me how very old she was, and I began to think of how dreadful it would be if she died. At that stage of my life I couldn't have imagined life without her.[11]

In spite of her very busy life, advancing age, and loneliness Peig was clearly a woman with a very strong personality who encouraged and loved company and knew how to enjoy herself, especially when away from home:

My grandmother loved having visitors, and loved talking with people. She felt at ease with people whether they were young or old. A nephew of hers (her brother's son) from Kilcatherine visited her fairly frequently. He and his wife and family of two girls lived in the old home in Kilcatherine. She spoke English to him. He and his wife are dead for many years.

My grandmother's best friend was Mrs Roger O'Sullivan from Barrakilla. She was about ten years younger than my grandmother and had originally come from Kilcatherine also. Her maiden name was Margaret Crowley. Surprisingly it was all English they spoke. In fact I never heard that lady speak Irish. She and my grandmother would go out together occasionally on a day trip to Kenmare. A bus travelled from Castletown to Kenmare once weekly and they would go off and have a great day together. She loved her glass of whiskey and they often talked about Mrs Guihan, Mrs Mihigan and Mrs Murphy, all of whom had pubs in Kenmare. She would be saving for this trip for a few weeks in advance. The savings came from the ten shillings weekly pension and was put away in a locked chest which she had in her bedroom. We often tried as children to get a peep into that chest, but it was like a little ritual when it was being opened – all of the children were banished from the room. Roger O'Sullivan had a sidecar (like the present day jaunting-cars) and sometimes he and his wife and my grandmother would go off on the sidecar for a day's outing. She loved these outings and she would be singing with delight.

Another regular visitor was Mike Sheehan (Micheál Ó Síocháin from Barrakilla, whom Tadhg Ó Murchú visited). They always spoke Irish to each other. We always listened to their conversations and were very pleased as we got older that we could understand what they were speaking about. They often spoke of the past, of the bad times, of their families and sometimes exchanged their health problems. If my grandmother complained of a pain or an ache Mike would say: 'Tánn tusa óg fós' ['You are young yet']. Mike was about six years older than my grandmother, so he would have been very old indeed at the time I remember him. He was very deaf and his sight was bad, but he made his way with help of a walking stick to our house. Because of his deafness he spoke in a very loud voice.[12]

From the many items of folklore collected from her which deal with the supernatural, death customs, local festivals, patterns and pilgrimages, etc., Peig Minihane could probably be described as a religious personality. However she certainly was not religious in the sense of being a typical conservative Catholic woman:

My grandmother said prayers every day and she would insist on the family rosary being said at night. She didn't go regularly to

Sunday Mass in her old age, but she would say her prayers at home at Mass time. However, her interest in what was happening round her was so intense that she always found it hard to really concentrate on her prayers. A prayer could go like this:

Hail Mary full of grace,
(Put out that devil of a dog)
The Lord is with thee,
Blessed art thou among women
(I hope the cows won't break into the meadow today).

And it went on and on like that. Sometimes she prayed in Irish and other times in English. I would say she wasn't an over-devout Catholic in the traditional style but she lived her religion and to me she was a marvellous Christian woman. Good Friday, though, was very special to her. She always fasted, took black tea, no butter, meat or eggs. Her only food on that day would be dry bread. She was always willing to help a neighbour in distress; she regularly visited sick people, and never missed a funeral. I cannot remember this but she told us that in earlier years when a neighbour died she would always be sent for to lay out the body.[13]

Her Catholic religious beliefs were obviously tempered by belief in many supernatural phenomena which would certainly have been frowned upon by the clergy of the time. In fact she seems to have had an unusual (for her time) lack of fear of the clergy as seen in one particular confrontation with a priest where her refusal to be bullied shows the power and control which she exerted over her own life when the situation demanded it:

As I said before Hannah was the only one that ever came home on a visit. Hannah was a very good melodeon player even as a young girl. At the time that Hannah was in her early twenties, there was a certain priest in Eyeries Parish whose name I cannot remember. He was very strict where young people were concerned and used to go out at night with a blackthorn stick chasing young courting couples. It was a custom at the time (and also much later in my young days) to have a 'ball night' in a house perhaps twice a year. The young people would get together to sing, dance and play some music. On a few occasions the priest came to these houses to break up the party and went as far at times as taking some of the girls' coats to the presbytery. He would keep the coats until they were collected by the owners. This priest didn't approve of people owning or playing musical instruments. He felt that by doing so they were getting people together to enjoy themselves. He publicly asked the parents to prevent their sons and daughters from playing music. My grandmother went to the priest and told him in no uncertain terms that her daughter had her full approval to play music, that in fact she herself had bought her the melodeon. She said she saw nothing wrong with what her daughter was doing and so it stood![14]

Peig's traditional mode of dress was very aptly described by her granddaughter and this helps us in building an overall picture of her personality and appearance:

My grandmother always wore traditional long dark skirts, a blouse and cardigan and a scarf on her head. I never remember seeing her go round bare-headed even in summer time. She wore a large black shawl when she was going somewhere. She never used a handbag but her money would be carried in her 'pocket'. This pocket, as she called it, was not part of her skirt but a small bag made from cotton material with two strings tied at the top which she put round her waist inside her skirt. There would be a small slit at the side of her skirt through which she put her hand to get to the pocket.

She wore slippers round the house but when she was going out she wore what she called her 'Cork Uppers'. At the time I didn't know where this name originated but I found out later that in actual fact the upper parts of these shoes were made in Cork city. They would be bought and taken to the local shoemaker who would sew the uppers on to a leather sole, all neatly stitched. So Cork Uppers was a very apt name indeed. These boots were always black, of very fine leather, with a lot of lacing, as they reached high up on the shin.

My grandmother had a few very colourful head scarves, one of which she wore inside her shawl when she was going out.[15]

Another vivid memory of her granddaughter's is the picture that remains in her mind of Peig's room with its furniture and simple decor:

My grandmother had a room downstairs in the old house. It was of average size, next to the kitchen. It was a very cold room, having no fireplace. At that time a fire would be the only means by which a room could be heated, as it was a few years later that electricity came to the area. We did not move to the new house until December 1952 when she moved into a large bright room, also on the ground floor.

In her old room, she had a large double bed with wooden ends. She always had two mattresses on the bed, one of which she called the 'tick'. She would occasionally take out this tick in the open air and soften up the feathers, and needless to say, we as children would love to jump and play on it. She had many patchwork quilts which she and her daughters made. These were all hand-stitched and must have taken a considerable time to make. During winter she would have two or three of those heavy quilts, as well as a few blankets on the bed. Certainly this amount of bed clothes was necessary because of the coldness of the room.

She also had beautiful works of crochet which I think were mainly done by her daughters. Much of this crochet was used as trimming on white pillow cases and on a valance which was round the frame of her bed. This valance had a twofold purpose. As well as being very decorative it served to cover and keep from view the many articles which were stored under the bed. The walls of the room, which were generally painted white, were lined with holy pictures and one large photo of her son Tim which she treasured. There was no floor covering but plain wooden boards which had to be scrubbed every week but she usually had a mat at her bedside.

There was a large table in the room which was often used by us as a homework table when we had to get away from the noise of the kitchen. Under this table she had a large wooden chest in which were kept her little personal belongings, letters from her family and any small savings which she might have. This chest was always locked. There was also another chest in the room in which were kept her bedclothes, works of crochet and some items of clothing etc. She took pride in keeping her room clean and tidy and she loved to show off her colourful bed. There was a long mantelpiece on one wall where her ornaments and holy water were kept.[16]

Peig remained healthy and active in her old age until her former strength and vigour began to fail in her last years:

My grandmother was in very good health until she was well over ninety. She hadn't a pain or an ache but she gradually got very feeble. At the age of about ninety she started to go senile. We would often find her talking to herself and it was always about her young days in Kilcatherine, and very often she would be speaking in Irish, as she did when she was a child.

I remember my grandmother as a woman who loved life, and took a tremendous interest in what was going on all round her.

She died peacefully in the spring of 1957.[17]

1 R. O'Dwyer, *Who Were My Ancestors – Genealogy (Family Trees) of the Eyeries Parish, Castletownbere, Co. Cork, Ireland* (Astoria 3, USA: Stevens Publishing Co., 1976), p. 101.

2 This account of her memories of her grandmother was written for me in longhand by Noreen Heaney (O'Sullivan), Glasnevin, Dublin (who was born and reared in Gurteen, Ardgroom, Co. Cork), Christmas, 1991.

3 *Ibid*.

4 O'Dwyer, *op cit*, p. 6.

5 Noreen Heaney's account.

6 O'Dwyer, *op cit*, p. 6–7.

7 Noreen Heaney's account.

8 *Ibid*. It may not have been unusual for women and even young girls in Peig Minihane's area to take part in rowing boats as Bríd Ní Shíocháin (69), of Inisfarnard testified to Tadhg Ó Murchú on 8/5/39 [IFC Vol. 623:255–56]: 'And every tide that came at the end of the night, there used to be two turf boats rowed into the island by us at the break of day. And it's many a turf boat I rowed myself – and that is no lie – and I a young girl. And when I used to row the boat, with the rowing, the hand grip of the oar used to blister my hand, and I have the blisters since – Look at them!'

9 Noreen Heaney's account.

10 *Ibid*.

11 *Ibid*.

12 *Ibid*.

13 *Ibid*.

14 *Ibid*.

15 *Ibid*.

16 *Ibid*.

17 *Ibid*.

# Tadhg Ó Murchú and Peig Minihane

When Tadhg Ó Murchú was collecting folklore around Ardgroom in June 1950, he called in to a man named Pádraig Ó Sé (Barley) in *Gort a' Leasa* near Ardgroom village. Having taken down a couple of short tales from him, Tadhg asked about any other people from the area who might be suitable informants:

> I wrote down two or three short tales from him – that was all he had – and I asked him about other old people – did he know of anyone around the place who would have Irish and knowledge of old times. He said to me that there was an old woman down by the side of the main road. She was Mrs John O'Sullivan, of the Minihane family (Driscoll) before she married. She was from Kilcatherine in the west. She was eighty-eight years old and she had great Irish, and he thought that maybe it might be worth my while to go and talk to her.[1]

*Tadhg O'Murchú, Kerry, 1936*

On 14 July, Tadhg Ó Murchú left Pádraig Ó Sé's house in *Gort a'*
*Leasa* and headed for the O'Sullivan house in Gurteen to meet
the old woman:

The old woman's house was a little east of the iron gate, up on a
little hillock which was on the side of the road, on the left hand side
as I went east – a fine slated house – it appeared to be well looked
after, as there were lots of flowers and little green trees growing
around it. I left the 'timber horse' [bicycle] at the side of the road
and I made my way to the house and went into the farmyard. A
young girl came out to the door to me as I headed towards the
house – a fine good-looking girl, light red [hair], around seventeen;
an active girl, strong, cheerful. I saluted her – I had no expectation
that she would have Irish, but she did – and I asked her if it was
here that such and such an old woman lived. She said that it was,
but that she was not in at the moment – that she was outside somewhere seeing to the hens and the turkeys, but that it wouldn't be
long until she would be coming. She said to me to go in and sit down.
I did, and I made my way to the rack and sat down. It was a fine
roomy kitchen, and it was nice and clean and tidy.

The young girl was baking bread – there was a very big range
there and the kitchen was very stuffy, very hot with the heat of the
fire and the warmth of the weather.

The young girl was a daughter of the man of the house. She
was in Coláiste Íde in Baile an Ghóilín [at school] she told me, but
that she was at home on holidays at the moment. Her father was a
foreman in the Board of Public Works and he was away at the moment taking part in some work scheme. Her mother and the rest
were out in the meadow working at hay, she said. She was a very
talkative girl – she wasn't a bit shy before the stranger.

It wasn't long until the old woman came in to us. She was a
tall, thin, dark woman, thin-faced, ruddy in her features, and she
was hearty and full of life. She wondered who the stranger man
was who had come to the house, but when the young girl explained
it to her she put a hundred welcomes before me. She had fluent
Irish – that fine old chat without rags or tassels that she got from
the old people who came before her – and she had short tales too
– many of them, as far as I could make out. I wrote down some of
the short tales from her, and the young girl was a great help to me.
She used to say to the grandmother not to be talking too quickly,
and to give me time to write down the things in the book – she was
a clever, understanding girl.

But I had a great evening in the company of the old woman – I loved listening to the clever chat she had, and to the stories she heard about the Famine. I had filled a bit of the notebook when I parted from her. It was mostly the heat of the kitchen that bothered me while I was writing down from her – I was in a lather of sweat. I said goodbye to the two of them around six o'clock, after promising the old woman that I would come to her again some other day and that I would take her picture.[2]

Tadhg was true to his word, because he paid another visit to Gurteen the next day:

I reached Gurteen around one o'clock and a great welcome was before me from the old woman, and from the rest of the household too – the young girl's mother – a generous, welcoming woman who was not too tall. She would be about forty-five, I thought – a well made, tidy woman, good-looking – with brown hair and a round face. She was on the Baile an Bhogaigh side [Co. Kerry] one night, she said, before she married, in the house of a relative of mine who lived there. The sea rose on them and they had to wait for a calm. They were very well looked after in the house, she said, and they had dancing and fun until morning there. There was a sister of the young girl there too, younger than herself – a fine, good-looking girl too – and two young boys: one of them grown up into a fine youth, and another one who was still at school – they were nice friendly boys – good-looking. They were just after coming in from the meadow and drinking tea when I burst in on them. I had to join them and have a cup of tea with them – fine lively tea and lovely oven bread.

When we had drunk the tea then, I thought that it would be a good idea to get the business of taking the picture over me while the sun was there and before the company would break up – they were in a hurry out to the hay and I wanted to take a picture of the whole household together.

But when the matter was mentioned to the old woman, she put her foot down straight away that she would not do it – she herself was too old, and bad complexioned now, she said, to have her picture taken. But we all went pleading with her to be in the picture, and she gave in to us in the end after much persuasion. She dressed herself up and came outside with the others and the picture was taken. She was very satisfied with herself then.

The mother and the boys went about the hay then, and the two girls stayed inside seeing to the cooking.

I gave the drop [of whiskey] to the old woman and she was delighted with it and I got twelve times its value in good blessings and prayers from her.

She was in great form for chatting then, and the two of us spent from then until around six o'clock in the evening on olden times and on short tales. I took down a good number of nice short tales from her during that time, and the young girls were a great help to get her going, and they had great interest in the work that we were doing. But we had a great evening, and I was very satisfied with the result of my labours. I said goodbye to the old woman then – she was a lovely poor old woman, and a woman who had a lot of old information and much old knowledge in her head – and to the two girls – they were lovely fine people, the whole lot of them – and I headed east to Bunaw.[3]

As old as she was, Tadhg's respect for Máiréad as a *seanchaí* grew when he next met her the following year on 9 June 1951 and she was still strong and healthy before him:

She put the depth of the winter over her without any flu or cold or pain touching her, she said, and she was working and as busy as ever she was.

From then on we drew down the old times, and I put lots of questions to her about certain facets of folklore, and there weren't many questions I put to her that she didn't answer with a short tale or some example. She is the most knowledgeable woman about these old matters that I ever met, and I wrote down a lot of information and short tales from her from then until around seven o'clock.

Believe me that we were both becoming tired of one another – or I was anyway – because to tell the truth, you couldn't tire the old woman – the old woman had great patience and she would not like to keep anything from me. But I myself was a bit agitated from the constant questioning and from the writing. A ceasefire was called then, and the old woman took a pinch of snuff – she takes snuff – and the woman of the house had a cup of tea ready for me – lovely tea and raisin bread baked in the oven. We spent another while storytelling after drinking the tea. It was heading for eight o' clock when I said goodbye to them and I was told that I would be welcome any time at all that I would like to call on her.[4]

Tadhg did call on her again on the 11,[5] 13,[6] 18,[7] 21 June[8] of that year and apparently, the old woman had a great interest in the business by now:

> Her son's wife tells me that she is looking forward now every day,
> to see if I am coming – she can't wait for me to arrive.[9]

And when Tadhg went to say goodbye to her on 24 September
1951,[10] she was very lonely:

> When it was time for us to part then, she said that she would be lonely
> now after me, because my visits were a great shortening on the day
> and the time, and she loved, as a pastime, to be recounting the af-
> fairs of olden times to the likes of me who was interested in them,
> but that we might see one another again before long with the help
> of God.[11]

When Tadhg was in Beara again the following year (4 September 1952), he went to see her and he collected 'some old accounts'
from her.[12] It is most likely that this was the last time they saw
one another.

---

1 IFC Vol. 1228:84–5.

2 IFC Vol. 1228:85–92.

3 Debora Kodish, 'Absent Gender, Silent Encounter' in S. Tower Hollis, Linda Pershing and
M. Jane Young, eds, *Feminist Theory and the Study of Folklore* (University of Illinois Press, 1993),
p. 42. She points out the convention which seems to have existed among folklorists of thinking of themselves as 'discovering' their informants: 'Like some wonder tales, folklorists' accounts of their own first encounters with traditional artists emphasise the magical or marvellous character of the event. The openings of such personal narratives often describe the diffi-
culties of the search, the obstacles overcome on the quest. Once encountered, the traditional
singer or storyteller often testifies to the special quality of the meeting. Thus, it is often noted
that storytellers as well as singers seemed to have been preparing for a folklorist's visit for
decades.' She considers it important that such conventions should be studied as 'significant
features of folklorists' own narratives'.

4 IFC Vol. 1228:150–55.

5 IFC Vol. 1228:682–75.

6 IFC Vol. 1228:687–88.

7 IFC Vol. 1228:698–99.

8 IFC Vol. 1228:729–31.

9 IFC Vol. 1228:744–46.

10 IFC Vol. 1228:698–99.

11 IFC Vol. 1338:5–8.

12 IFC Vol. 1338:6–7.

# Tadhg Ó Murchú's Visits
## as Remembered by Noreen Heaney

The young girl present when Tadhg first visited Máiréad was her granddaughter Noreen who remembers well the sessions for which she was present:

Yes, I remember the sessions with Tadhg Ó Murchú. Perhaps not all of them, as I would have been in Gurteen only during holiday time from school. She also had a few visits from Seán Ó Súilleabháin, who was a native of Ardea in the Tuosist Parish. I cannot remember whether these visits took place before or after Tadhg's visits. I remember the day (which is mentioned in the notes by Tadhg) when I was in the kitchen baking bread, and they had a great long session together.

She loved these visits and always looked forward to the next one. She was a born storyteller, and to find somebody who not only listened, but also wrote what she had to say must have been absolutely great for her. She loved having people round her and enjoyed the attention which these visits offered her. Telling ghost stories was her favourite pastime, but where the family was concerned she did not get the attention to these stories which she would have liked. No doubt we loved listening to them but my mother felt that we as children should not be listening to all these scary stories. She herself was terrified in the dark as a result of hearing the same stories over and over again. This is why Tadhg Ó Murchú has a footnote saying that my grandmother would not tell where the graves of the dead were *'ar eagla go scéithfeadh an gearrchaile uirthi'* ['in case the girl would tell on her'].

There was a distance of about two miles between our house and the village. There were several haunted spots along that road according to my grandmother. We often had to cycle this distance in the dark of night. I can still feel the terror which I had in my heart as I pedalled furiously to get past all these haunted spots, where the dead were seen or where strange sounds were heard. First of all there was the place where the black hare ran under the horse's legs as he carried the priest to give the last rites to a dying person. Then there was the haunted gravel pit, and as you broke out in perspiration you thought that if you got past Hartnett's gate where all the weird noises were heard that the worst was over.

There was a hollow between rocks not far from our house which was called Poll Mór [Big Hole]. My grandmother told us that many people were buried together there at the time of the Famine. She had many many stories of haunted houses, but I would not think she told many of those stories to Tadhg. She believed, as did many old people that if a house was built on an old path that it was haunted.

When Tadhg Ó Murchú visited our house he always sat at the table (C), where he had a comfortable position for writing. My gran's usual position was A, but she sat at B when speaking to Tadhg. She sat fairly close to him on a high chair with her back to the wall beside the fire. I remember this very well, as my grandmother had a special chair at the other side of the fireplace but she always changed her position when Tadhg came, in order to be closer to where he sat.

When Tadhg started taking notes from my grandmother she was inclined to ramble on without stopping – at the beginning. You would have to ask her to stop so that he could get it all written. He would ask her questions, and usually the answers came pretty fast. Sometimes she would stop and think for a minute or two and then proceed. As time went on she knew exactly when to stop, and she would be watching him write and would wait until he was ready to continue further.

What I remember most about these visits was the joy it gave my grandmother to sit there and relate all these stories. My grandmother was very sad indeed when Tadhg's visits were over.

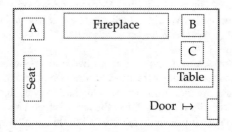

# Additional Folklore from Peig Minihane

## as Remembered by Noreen Heaney

*The following are some items of folklore which Noreen Heaney remembered hearing from her grandmother, Peig Minihane. Noreen sent me this material in January 1992. The English translations (in square brackets) of items in Irish were added by myself.*

### 1. Irish words and expressions

If somebody died she would never say, 'God rest his soul'. It would always be, *'Beannacht Dé lena anam'*.

If you wore a new garment she would say, *'Go mairir is go gcaithir é'* ['May you live to wear it'], and if she were speaking to me or to my sisters she would add, *'Agus go bpósfaidh tú fear ann'* ['And may you marry a man there'].

If you found something which was lost she would say, *'Go dtuga Dia radharc na súl duit'* ['May God give you the sight of your eyes'].

She had several old sayings *(seanfhocail)* which she used as the occasion arose. For example if you were upset about something she would say, *'Is mairg a bháitear in am an anaithe (anfa) mar tagann an ghrian i ndiaidh na fearthainne.'* ['Pity those who die during the storm because the sun comes out after the rain.']

If you weren't up to scratch in doing things she might reprimand you and say, *'Ní hé lá na gaoithe lá na scolb'* ['The windy day is not the thatching day'].

If she heard people speak badly of others she would say, *'Is minic a bhris béal duine a shrón'* ['It's often that a person's mouth broke her/his nose'] – and it went on and on.

## 2. Magpies

When she saw magpies she never failed to say the old rhyme:

| | |
|---|---|
| *Aon don mhí-ádh,* | [One for sorrow, |
| *Dó don mheidhir,* | Two for joy, |
| *Is ceathair don chrá,* | And four for torment, |
| *Cúig don airgead,* | Five for money |
| *Sé don ór,* | Six for gold, |
| *Seacht don rún,* | Seven for the secret, |
| *Fé chlúid go deo.* | Never told.] |

To this day if I see magpies I always think of that rhyme and if one appears I am hoping that the second one will come along for good luck.

## 3. A Riddle in Irish

She had Irish riddles, one of which I remember:

| | |
|---|---|
| *Chomh bán le bainne,* | [As white as milk, |
| *Chomh dearg le fuil,* | As red as blood, |
| *Chomh hard le falla,* | As high as a wall, |
| *Chomh milis le mil.* | As sweet as honey.] |

I cannot remember the answer. [An apple up in a tree.]

## 4. Daniel O'Connell

She had a little story about Daniel O'Connell, who on one occasion went to England, and according to her story there was a plot to poison him. He was sitting at table one day when the maid came in carrying a tray with a drink for O'Connell. The maid was Irish and she knew that there was poison in the drink. As she placed the tray on the table she started to sing in a low voice, as if she were enjoying her work. The words went as follows:

| | |
|---|---|
| *'A Dhónaill Uí Chonail* | ['Oh Daniel O'Connell |
| *An dtuigeann tú Gaelainn?'* | Do you understand Irish?'] |

He replied:

| | |
|---|---|
| *'Tuigim go cliste, a chailín* | ['I understand well, oh girl |
| *ó Éirinn,* | from Ireland, |
| *Agus cad is baol dom?'* | And what is my danger?'] |

She sang on as she continued her work:

| | |
|---|---|
| *'Tá blaise den tsalann* | ['There is a taste of salt |
| *Sa ghloine sin taobh leat* | In that glass beside you |
| *Is ding dong de-da-ró* | And ding dong de-de da-ro |
| *Ding dong dé ró* | Ding dong de ro |
| *Ding dong de-da-ró* | Ding dong de-da-ro |
| *Is ding dong dé ró.'* | Ding dong de ro.'] |

### 5. *'All who came and went will go' (a cantefable)*

Not far from our house stood the ruins of an old building. It was at the side of the main road. Part of the roof was intact and there was one big room which had an open fireplace. When itinerants were passing by they sometimes stayed there overnight and they would light a big fire on the hearth. My grandmother often brought them food, and would sit and talk with them.

One day she was walking along the road with my sister and they saw one of the itinerants in our field getting some firewood. My sister cannot remember what remark exactly she herself made, but she feels that she must have suggested that the itinerant should be asked to get out of our field. My grandmother then went on to tell her the story of another tinker who was once caught stealing furze in a farmer's field. The farmer came along and attacked the tinker and this is what the tinker said:

| | |
|---|---|
| *Imeoidh a dtiocfaidh is a dtáinig,* | [All who came and went will leave, |
| *Ach ní imeoidh an grást ó Dhia.* | But God's grace will stay. |
| *Imeoidh mise agus tusa ón áit seo,* | You and I will leave this place, |
| *Is beidh an aiteann ag fás 'nár ndiaidh.* | And the furze will be growing after us.] |

And my grandmother added: *'Agus dúirt an feirmeoir leis aiteann a thógaint aon uair a bhí sí uaidh'* ['And the farmer told him to take furze any time he wanted it'].

When she wanted to get her point across she always managed to have a little story to relate.

## 6. Saint John's Day

There were certain feast days to which my grandmother gave great attention and she liked to adhere to the old customs associated with these feasts. Saint John's Day was a special one. I think it falls round 20 June. We had to light bonfires beside the field where the potatoes were planted. The position of the bonfire depended on which direction the wind was blowing, because it was important that the smoke from the bonfire blew right over the crop.

## 7. May Day

The first of May, or *Lá Bealtaine* [May Day] as she called it, was very special. It was customary to get up before sunrise to bring in the 'summer'. In her younger days she would bring in branches from the various trees and keep these in the house until the following year. When I was young my father continued that tradition, and if he wasn't at home my grandmother made sure that we got up to bring in the summer some hours before going to school. She used to recite the little *dán*:

> *Thugamar féin an samhradh linn,*
> We ourselves brought the summer with us,
> *Thugamar linn é is cé bhainfidh dínn é?*
> We brought it with us and who will take it from us?
> *Thugamar féin an samhradh linn.*
> We ourselves brought the summer with us.
> *Samhradh samhradh bainne na ngamhna,*
> Summer summer the milk of the calves,
> *Thugamar féin an samhradh linn,*
> We ourselves brought the summer with us,
> *Samhradh buí fé luí na gréine,*
> A yellow summer under the beating sun,
> *Thugamar féin an samhradh linn.*
> We ourselves brought the summer with us.
> *Cuileann is coll is trom is cárthann,*
> Holly and hazel and elder and rowan,
> *Thugamar féin an samhradh linn,*
> We ourselves brought the summer with us,
> *Fuinseog gléigeal Béal an Átha,*
> Shimmering bright ash from the Mouth of the Ford,

> *Thugamar féin an samhradh linn.*
> We ourselves brought the summer with us.

This was a *dán* with several verses, but I cannot remember the remainder of the poem.

## 8. Good Friday

My grandmother always fasted on Good Friday. Her only food would be dry bread and black tea. It was either on Ash Wednesday or Good Friday that she always brought in a twig, put it in the fire and when it was nicely singed she used to make the Sign of the Cross on our foreheads with it.

## 9. Saint Stephen's Day

She always looked forward to Saint Stephen's Day when the wren boys went out round the neighbourhood dressed in bright clothes. They would sing songs as they approached each house. My grandmother always asked them to sing the 'Wren Song', and if they did she would pay them well for their efforts. She told us that in earlier years the wrenboys would always have a dead wren hanging on the bush and sometimes they might have spent a whole week beforehand looking for the wren. They wouldn't get money then unless they had the wren. I remember a few lines of her song:

> The wren the wren the king of all birds,
> Saint Stephen's Day he was caught in the furze,
> Although he was little his honour was great,
> Cheer up oh landlady and give us a trate (treat).
> Michael O'Sullivan is a dacent (decent) man,
> To his house we brought the wran (wren),
> Up with the kettle and down with the pot,
> Give us an answer and let us be off.

She also had an Irish version of that song but I can remember only a few lines (as it sounded):

> *Dreoilín a fuaireas-sa thíos ar an Inse,*
> A wren I got down on the river meadow,

*Fé bhrat carraige is carbhat síoda air,*
Under the shade of a rock with a silk tie on it,
*Thugas-sa chughaibhse é, 'lánúin an tí seo,*
I brought it to you, couple of this house
*Is go mba seacht mb'fhearr um an dtaca seo 'rís sibh.*
And may you be seven times better the next time round.

### 10. The man in the moon

My grandmother used to tell us the story of the man in the moon. She said he is carrying a bush on his shoulder. This man was placed on the moon as a punishment for his sins. On one occasion during his lifetime he stole a bush from a neighbour's field, and so he had to carry it for all eternity on the moon, for all the world to see.

### 11. Teeth

If a tooth fell out during our childhood my grandmother would make us throw the tooth back over our shoulders and bless ourselves.

### 12. Spiders

She would never let us kill a spider. She said they were sacred.

### 13. Wearing clothes for the dead

Customs relating to the dead were very important to her – especially the customs in relation to the wearing of peoples' clothes after their death. One of these customs was that if a person died, his or her clothes would have to be worn to Mass on three successive Sundays, and if the dead person didn't have reasonably good clothes, new garments would sometimes be bought. It didn't matter if these clothes weren't the right size for the wearer. The important thing was that they would be the proper size for the dead person. I have never heard of this peculiar custom being in any other part of the country and it was beginning to die out when I was young.

For a while then this custom was replaced by another which was even crazier. People put the dead person's clothes in a suitcase which they brought to the church (leaving it inside the church door) for three Sundays. My grandmother didn't approve of this at all. She felt people were taking the easy way out and were not being loyal to the dead.

## 14. Field names

My grandmother loved the farm animals and each cow had a name. She also had a name for every field in the farm – mostly Irish names, and some of these names were very suitable for the size and position of the field. To mention but a few, she called one field *Páirc a' Bhóthair*, another *Páirc Láir*, others still were *Páirc Mhór, Grafa Mór, Leaca Mór, Cnocán a' Chró, Páirc a' Gheata, Lúib a' Gheata, Páirc Pheter*. Perhaps these fields had already been named before my grandmother came to Gurteen. I do not know.

# Women as Storytellers

In the introduction to the book *Women's Folklore, Women's Culture* (1985), the editors Rosan A. Jordan and Susan Kalcik point out that until recently, folklorists have largely confined their attention to performances that belong to the world of men and which take place in a very public, demonstrative and competitive manner, and that they have ignored folklore conducted in the privacy of the home. Genres such as 'personal experience narratives' and popular beliefs have been dismissed as 'minor genres' or 'old wives' tales' or 'just gossip'.[1] Although the neglect of performances conducted in the privacy of the home would not apply to Irish folklore scholarship, the principles behind what Jordan and Kalcik say, do, I believe, apply to the study of folklore here in the past.

This type of bias must be taken as an example of 'sexism', described by Bernard (1971) as:

> the unquestioned, unexamined, and unchallenged acceptance of the belief that the world as it looked to men was the only world, that the way of dealing with it that men had created was the only way, that the values men had evolved were the only ones.[2]

And as regards the type of material considered to be of value by both the ordinary people and folklorists:

> these recognised, usually male, genres assume the status of 'legitimate folklore genres'. Female expressive forms either fit the male mold or they are relegated to a non-legitimate, less-than-expressive category.[3]

It would seem important to enquire then as to what way folklore studies have viewed women in the past:

> Folklore studies then, like anthropological studies, have described women as men see [or don't see] them. A tendency to see the world

in male terms has influenced what kind of data folklorists have looked for and from whom, and also what data they have actually collected and from whom.[4]

In regard to female storytellers in Ireland and elsewhere the American folklorist Stith Thompson had the following to say:

In Ireland the actual delivery of the stories seems to be a prerogative of the men, though women certainly know them and teach them to their children. On the other hand, tales reported from East Prussia were taken down from women though this may be because the collector of these stories is a woman.[5]

In his Sir John Rhys Memorial Lecture (1946) Séamus Ó Duilearga made the following, now widely accepted, observations regarding women storytellers in Ireland:

The recital of Ossianic hero-tales was almost without exception restricted to men. 'A woman fiannaí or a crowing hen!' the proverb runs. There are exceptions to this rule, but still the evidence is unmistakable that the telling by women of Finn-tales was frowned upon by the men.

Seanchas, genealogical lore, music, folk-prayers, were, as a rule, associated with women; at any rate they excelled the men in these branches of tradition. While women do not take part in the storytelling, not a word of the tale escapes them, and if their relatives or close friends make any slip or hesitate in their recital, it is a not uncommon experience of mine to hear the listening woman interrupt and correct the speaker.[6]

The American folklorist Clodagh Brennan Harvey more recently (1992) came to the same basic conclusions about women storytellers:

first, that women participated less than men; second, that men rather than women tended to be the narrators of the longer, multi-episodic tales, such as Märchen and hero tales (sean-scéalta and scéalta gaisce, respectively); third, that it was also considered inappropriate for women to tell hero tales, particularly those of the Fenian cycle (finnscéalta); and fourth, as a corollary to these points, that men and women usually went visiting separately. There were notable exceptions to the supposed inferiority of women as narrators of the long stories (such as famed woman narrator, Peig Sayers)[7]

However having said that, Brennan Harvey points out that:

there is a general lack of information about women storytellers, the types of stories women told, and the contexts in which they participated in the tradition.[8]

It has also been strongly argued that the range of subjects on which information has been collected from women is very limited. What this means is that the genres of women's folklore which have been accepted have done so because they fit into whatever happens to be the prevailing image of women.[9]

Another point of major importance which limits our knowledge of women as bearers and transmitters of oral tradition in general is the fact that there were no full-time female collectors working for the Irish Folklore Commission. As regards the particular collection under study here, one must speculate as to whether the material collected or the interaction between collector and informant would have been different if the collector had been a woman. It is important to bear in mind that the intrusion of any collector would obviously influence the subjects that the informant would discuss and that collecting done in the 'private sphere' of our informant, Peig Minihane, in conversation with her female contemporaries or family would probably bring much other valuable material to light:

The gender of the folklore fieldworker influences what he or she looks for; it affects his or her relationship with informants, and what he or she is ready and able to see and hear and understand as important.[10]

However, the setting up of an intimate environment for the purpose of collecting folklore is not easy to achieve for someone who is not a relative of the informant; is not of the same gender; or has not the time required to create ideal collecting situations. In any case, in the social and academic climate of the fifties in Ireland this would not have been considered to be important.

Furthermore we simply do not know enough about what the occasions for telling stories were for women. Brennan Harvey also points out the importance of the lack of female collectors and the absence of information concerning purely female gatherings during which opportunities for storytelling must surely have been available and taken advantage of:

Generally, it has simply never been possible to document all the aspects of the tradition or all the social situations of which storytelling was a part. In fact, there is woefully little *in situ* documentation of Irish storytelling at all. More specifically, and potentially far more important, I have encountered almost no references to women collectors. Setting aside Lady Augusta Gregory's unique contribution to Irish folklore and literature, since the early days of folklore collecting, the overwhelming majority of the collectors have been men. This has important implications in terms of what we know about women's storytelling. Although it was not invariably the case, it was generally customary for men and women to go *ar cuairt* [visiting] separately; and we really have no exact information as to what kinds of stories women told in the gatherings in which only women participated, except to assume that they continued to follow to some degree the traditional norms of appropriateness for storytelling. In addition to the groups involved in nightly visiting, there may have been other such all-female groups. For example, the collector Seán Ó hEocaidh described to me a form of transhumance practised in Donegal until about one hundred years ago. During summer, groups of women would take their cattle from the lowlands up to the mountains where they lived in small cabins (*bothóga*) built for this purpose. Seán said that he knew they had *céilís* and sang songs, but there is no record of whether or not they told stories. It seems extremely probable to me, given such isolated social conditions, that they would have. Even if a collector had been present in either of these two kinds of settings, the presence of a male collector in such groups would unquestionably alter the dynamics of group interaction and the nature of the stories told. What I wish to suggest here is highly speculative, but it is possible that women in such contexts did not find it necessary to conform completely to the societal norms for behaviour in 'mixed' groups, as they do not in our own culture; that more women may have narrated than did so in mixed company; and that more may have ventured to tell the kinds of stories usually associated with men: hero tales, Märchen and, possibly, even off-colour or obscene material. We simply have no *in situ* docu-

147

mentation of storytelling in such settings upon which to judge. This situation represents an intriguing ethnographic problem, but one which, at this time, is undoubtedly beyond amelioration.[11]

There is some evidence that certain all female gatherings took place in Peig Minihane's district during her lifetime. Tadhg Ó Murchú collected the following piece of information from Bríd Ní Shíocháin who was born and reared on the little island of Inisfarnard, just off the Point of Kilcatherine near where Peig Minihane was born:

> but what we used be doing every night – us girls – was carding wool and spinning. Oh there were plenty sheep in the island! There were plenty sheep in the island always and wool and thread – that's what kept the clothes on them. We used be spinning and carding every night and knitting.[12]

However we are not really concerned here with whether or not women told Märchen and hero-tales during any such all female gatherings because other types of narrative associated particularly with women must be of equal importance with genres considered to be mainly the property of male storytellers:

> folklore is an important means of expressing attitudes, ideology and world view, whether consciously or unconsciously … Women's folklore tells us things that social strictures or psychological representations prevent women from otherwise saying – things at variance with the official ideal of culture. Narratives sometimes express ideas and feelings that would never emerge from a questionnaire or an interview or they may express them more powerfully.[13]

Although Tadhg Ó Murchú was a very accomplished collector of folklore, he was still very much under the influence of his superiors in the Irish Folklore Commission as to what type of material he should collect and the commission was very much a male dominated body. We have the advantage of the text of many of Tadhg's own questions to our informant which give us an indication of how he may have led her with his line of questioning. We also have the evidence of her granddaughter of how Tadhg prevented her from 'rambling on', which may mean talking about things which he did not consider to be important.[14] One must question some of Tadhg's decisions not to collect material from certain people on the grounds that they had nothing important to say. For example, because one old woman from Eyeries – who had spent many years in America – had no information on the topics about which he questioned her, he did not bother with her any further:

> The old woman came down to me in a little while. A hardy little woman – no one would imagine her to be over ninety-seven years old. She had her rosary in her hand. She saluted me in Irish and it's she who spoke it beautifully. She spent a good spell of her life beyond in America, she told me. There are not many old women or men in Beara who have not spent some part of their lives there. I began to question her about olden times – and especially about the Famine times – but it's little knowledge she had about any of those times. I think that her time in America scattered her memory of olden times. I had a long chat with her but I didn't learn anything worth mentioning.[15]

It is difficult to believe that a woman who had lived for ninety-seven years and spent her life in Ireland and America would have nothing of importance to say! This type of exclusion of women is an example of the 'tunnel vision' of folklore scholarship[16] which existed at that time and still does to a large extent:

> This kind of bias, and the fact that until recently most fieldworkers were male and did not have free access to women's culture, have naturally affected folklore research and fieldwork, in its conceptualisation, in its application and in the interpretation of data. In general, this male orientation has meant that women's expressive culture is ignored or viewed as insignificant and limited.[17]

In spite of the inevitable deficiencies of this collection, resulting from the types of bias mentioned above, it must be said that Tadhg Ó Murchú collected much valuable and unique material from Peig Minihane; that he had great admiration for her knowledge, view of life and beliefs; and that she in turn responded with great enthusiasm to his questioning and enjoyed the chance to share many of her beliefs and experiences with him.

The study of folklore in Ireland from the point of view of women has not been tackled or even seriously considered by most scholars up to now. However, the problems and some of the possible goals for those studying women's folklore here have been very aptly summed up by the Irish folklorist Anne O'Connor:

> Detailed analysis of gender and class still awaits sufficient attention in Irish folklore, just as in other areas of Irish scholarship. The oral traditional material itself, however, must first be uncovered. The individual women and their contributions have yet to be brought to light and appreciated within the Irish context. And certainly the questioning of given norms and the recognition of subjectivity in both the collecting and study of folklore are essential for our further understanding of folk tradition.[18]

I hope that this collection will go some small way towards 'uncovering' this important material.[19]

1 R. A. Jordan and S. J. Kalcik, 'Introduction – Women's Folklore, Women's Culture' in R. A. Jordan and S. J. Kalcik, eds, *Women's Folklore, Women's Culture* (University of Pennsylvania Press, 1985), p. ix.

2 J. Bernard, *Women and the Public Interest* (Chicago, 1971), p. 37.

3 C. R. Farrer, 'Introduction: Women and Folklore, Images and Genres', *Journal of American Folklore* 88 (1975a): p. xv–xvi.

4 Jordan & Kalcik, *op. cit.*, p. xi.

5 S. Thompson, *The Folktale* (University of California Press, 1946), p. 408.

6 J. H. Delargy, 'The Gaelic Storyteller', *Proceedings of the British Academy* 31 (1946), p. 7.

7 C. Brennan Harvey, *Contemporary Irish Traditional Narrative – The English Language Tradition* (University of California Press, 1992), p. 47–8.

8 *Ibid.*, p. 48.

9 Jordan & Kalcik, *op. cit.*, p. x.

10 *Ibid.*

11 Brennan Harvey, *op. cit.*, p. 48–9.

12 IFC Vol. 623:257 – collected by Tadhg Ó Murchú (8/9/39) from Bríd Ní Shíocháin (69), Fay, Kilcatherine.

13 A. O'Connor, 'Review – Women's Folklore, Women's Culture', *Béaloideas* 54–55 (1986–87), p. 302.

14 An account of her memories of her grandmother written for me (Christmas 1991) in longhand by Noreen Heaney (O'Sullivan), Glasnevin, Dublin (who was born and reared
in Gurteen, Ardgroom, Co. Cork).

15 Diary of Tadhg Ó Murchú – IFC Vol. 637:62–63.

16 M. Jane Young and K. Turner, 'Challenging the Canon: Folklore Theory Reconsidered
from Feminist Perspectives' in S. Tower Hollis, Linda Pershing and M. Jane Young,
eds, *Feminist Theory and the Study of Folklore* (University of Illinois Press, 1993), p. 10.

17 Jordan and Kalcik, *op. cit.*, p. xi.

18 A. O'Connor, *op. cit.*, p. 302.

19 Two important collections of folklore collected from Irish women have been published
since this chapter was originally written. One is a bilingual book of *seanchas* by a well-known
Donegal female storyteller (G. W. MacLennan, *Seanchas Annie Bhán – the Lore of Annie Bhán*,
[The Seanchas of Annie Bhán Publications Committee, 1977]), and the other is a collection
of stories in Irish (including a CD or video) by a contemporary female storyteller from Dunquin, Co. Kerry. (B. Almqvist and R. Ó Cathasaigh, *Ó Bhéal na Bhab – Cnuas-Scéalta Bhab Feir-
téir* [Radio na Gaeltachta agus Coláiste Mhuire gan Smál, 2002]).

# The Decline of Irish in Kilcatherine Parish

Although the 1851 census was the first to obtain information about the numbers of Irish speakers, Garret FitzGerald, using information from the 1881 census (and to a lesser extent less satisfactory data from the 1851 and 1861 censuses) succeeded in calculating the 'approximate minimum level of Irish-speaking in respect of successive new generations of young people in different parts of Ireland (the geographical unit being the barony) from around 1770–1870'.[1] Table 1 shows his estimates of the percentage of Irish speakers of different age groups in the Barony of Bear.

TABLE 1
*Estimated minimum level (%) of Irish-speaking among successive decennial cohorts in the Barony of Bear, born 1771–1871.*

| BORN | 1861–71 | 1851–61 | 1841–51 | 1831–41 | 1821–31 |
|------|---------|---------|---------|---------|---------|
| % | 66 | 84 | 90 | 93 | 95 |

| BORN | 1811–21 | 1801–11 | 1791–1801 | 1781–91 | 1771–81 |
|------|---------|---------|-----------|---------|---------|
| % | 97 | 100 | 100 | 99 | 99 |

Apart from these very valuable estimates we must depend on contemporary accounts for any direct information prior to the 1851 census. Frederick Roper wrote an important report on the labourers who were working in the Allihies mines before the Great Famine. Referring to an enquiry he made in 1841, he says:

> These mines are in a very isolated situation, and the persons there seldom extend their journeys beyond Castletown, about six miles. I had great difficulty in understanding them, or making myself understood; indeed I could not have got on at all without an interpreter; they mostly spoke Irish only, and many of them understood but little English.
>
> The people of these mines are very poor, poorly clad and seldom have more than two meals a day … those of potatoes, with, but

seldom, milk; of course some of the miners live better, but generally speaking they barely exist and, notwithstanding this great
scantiness of food, all, old and young, look very well and healthy,
and certainly do not show any the slightest symptoms, in their personal appearance, of being scantily fed. There were but very few
children. Captain Reed says he does not like them so young, they
are more trouble than they are worth. There is a doctor resident in
the neighbourhood, paid by the proprietor and the miners. There
is a day-school also, on the principle of the national school; but it is
frequented only by the children of the mechanics and better class
of miners and not by any children who are in the habit of working
at the mines. A Wesleyan preacher attends on Sundays in the school-
room, but with very trifling exceptions, the miners and workpeople
here are Roman Catholics; there is a chapel about two miles from
the mines.[2]

Whatever credence can be placed in Roper's views about the speaking of Irish among the labourers in the mines, and there is no obvious reason to doubt their accuracy, we have very little other information from this remote part of Beara from that time. Only 4,278
people out of a population of 89,986 in the Barony of Bear, according to the 1851 census, admitted that they could not speak English.
When one considers that these monoglots would include many
old people together with young people who might later learn English, one might expect Irish to decline very rapidly after that. Indeed, this did not happen because, fifty years later, according to
the 1901 census, there were 193 people without English and 5,774
who had Irish and English in the Castletown Rural District alone.
It is important to remember that this district did not include Kilcaskan or Glengarriff District Electoral Divisions, two of the stron-
gest Irish-speaking areas, which would have been included in
the Barony of Bear figures for 1851. It has been claimed that the
figures for the numbers of Irish speakers were too low in the 1851
Census,[3] and it would indeed appear that the figures for 1861 –
showing a rise in the number of Irish speakers – were more realis-
tic as regards Beara, Garret FitzGerald's figures would certainly
seem to bear this out.

Whatever about the accuracy of the 1851 and 1861 censuses
regarding Irish speakers, it seems certain that Irish was still the
home language of the country people during the childhood of

Peig Minihane. At the same time, it is clear from Table 4 (p. 161) that English was making considerable inroads in Beara from 1861 on. If we look at the dramatic drop in the population of Kilcatherine (Eyeries) Parish between 1841 and 1911 (see Table 5, p. 162) we get some insight into the reasons for the decline of Irish. It would seem that the Great Famine must have been responsible for at least some of the despair of the people which contributed to the abandonment of their language. Although the Allihies mines were in operation from 1812 until around 1875, they had been in decline for some time before they were eventually closed.[4]

On looking through Riobeard O'Dwyer's book on the genealogy of Eyeries Parish (the civil parish of Kilcatherine) one is especially struck by the number of people who emigrated to Butte, Montana.[5] David M. Emmons says that 1,700 people emigrated from Eyeries Parish to America between 1870 and 1915. Of these 1,138 (707 men and 431 women) went to Butte.[6] Frequently one member of a family after another left, with only the parents remaining in the end. This must have placed great pressure on parents to ensure that their children would be able to speak English. This emphasis on learning English is obvious from the words of our informant, Peig Minihane:

> While I was at school I didn't speak a word of Irish. It was a master we had at first, and when the new school was built then (in Kilcatherine) he was sent west to Urhan. Stephen McCarthy was the first master we had. He was from Canfie.
>
> I suppose I was ten years before I ever went to school. We used be learning the English at home – the boys who came before me, they used be learning English.[7]

In spite of the great pressure to speak English there were still children coming to school who had very little of that language according to Peig:

> Oh, there were many of them coming, no doubt, who had no word of English except broken English. When some of them came – poor girls who had nobody to teach them – they used only have broken English. But the mistress used to be questioning them …
>
> 'Tell me now,' said the mistress – the mistress was an outsider, who was in Eyeries, and she used to walk every day from Eyeries

to Kilcatherine and a little dog with her – Tiny. She had no Irish no
doubt. Right. She asked the little one the first day she came to school
… 'Where does the man wear his hat? Is it on his leg or his hand?'
'On him head,' said she.[8]

Peig Minihane herself was very friendly with a neighbour, Margaret Crowley, who was married to Roger O'Sullivan of Barra Coille. They were both from the Kilcatherine district and Margaret Crowley was also a fluent speaker of Irish.[9] Indeed, Margaret Crowley's mother was one of the people recorded in the census returns of 1901 as having no English.[10] Although these two women remained great friends all their lives and went everywhere together, they were not in the habit of speaking Irish to one another.[11]

When Peadar Ó hAnnracháin visited Rinn Troisc (Allihies Parish) in 1906 he was made very conscious of the loss of respect for their language among Irish-speakers even in that very remote townland:

Everyone there has fluent Irish but they are ashamed to speak it, the creatures.[12]

It is not surprising, then, that Irish had no status at all in Rinn Troisc Primary School as Peadar found out when he visited it at that time:

I visited the school on Tuesday, and that was the first time that Irish was mentioned there. However long the school is there all that has happened is the establishment of English and the death of Irish. There was nobody who could recognise the Irish letters, even the teacher, although she could speak it fluently. There isn't a prayer or creed in Irish there, but a little start was made that day.[13]

And the attitude of the Catholic Church seemed even worse if what one old woman told Peadar is true:

Eisc a' Bháid is below the school and Gortahig to the east of it. In Eisc a' Bháid I was speaking to an old woman on my way home from the school on Tuesday. She told me that a priest who was there when she was a young woman often struck people when they would not speak English to him.

He beat them with a stick! This priest is still alive. And still now there is a priest there and he heard the woman's confession in her house a while ago, but she said: 'It would have been as well for me to go out into the field and tell my story to a stone. We did not understand a word from one another.'[14]

Although Tadhg Ó Murchú met good Irish speakers everywhere in Eyeries Parish in 1939, most of them were old people and it was usually the case that young women, who were married into houses in which Irish was still spoken, did not themselves speak the language. For example, when he visited Eoghan Ó Sé (Stokes) in Droinn a' Bhogaigh on 28 April 1939: 'The old man and the son had fluent Irish, but the young woman did not seem to have a word.'[15]

It was almost the exact same story in six other houses visited by Tadhg – the old people and their son being Irish speakers, but the young married woman being unable (or possibly unwilling) to speak the language. He did not mention any case where the opposite was true – the young woman to be an Irish speaker and her husband having English only. Whatever social pressures were on young women to totally abandon Irish or deny knowledge of it, this did not bode well for its future. This seems all the more regrettable when one considers that by far the greater number of monoglot Irish speakers according to 1901 and 1911 censuses were women (see Tables 6 and 7). It may very well have been that young married women felt very strongly the burden of seeing to their children's education which, more than anything else at that time, meant making sure that they had a good knowledge of English. This tendency of women to follow the example of priests, teachers, shopkeepers etc. and take up the language of social advancement and respectability seems to have been a common phenomenon. The social pressures on women which led to it have been discussed in detail by Brighid Ní Mhóráin in her important work on the decline of Irish in the Iveragh Peninsula, Co. Kerry.[16]

As the Barony and Rural District were much too large as units in order to get detailed information on the status of Irish in our informant's district, I undertook detailed examination of the census returns from all the townlands of Kilcatherine Parish for 1901 and 1911 (see Tables 6 and 7). These forms are not available for years previous to 1901 or after 1911. As can be seen from the figures, the vast majority of Peig Minihane's neighbours would have had the ability to speak Irish when she was a young woman, although we can't say how many of them were actually still speaking it among themselves.

In these two censuses, people only had the choice of being recorded as having 'Irish Only' or 'Irish and English'. For instance, they did not have the choice of being recorded as having 'English Only' when this was the case – the relevant space on the form would have to be left empty or a line drawn through it. Sometimes this space would be left empty in the case of a child under one year old, although all other children in the household might be Irish speakers. Usually, this space being left empty meant that the person had 'English Only' but it is clear that it would be incorrect to interpret it in this way in all cases. Sometimes 'English Only' was actually written in this space even though this was not officially permitted, but in such cases it was clear that English was being spoken to the child in question or at least that English was the language preferred by the parents for their children.

There is another problem in interpreting the returns for the 1911 census in the opinion of Brendan Adams:

> Later as Irish rose in public estimation, there ceased to be any reason for concealing the fact that one could speak it, and by 1911 distortion went the other way, for by then many who were claiming to be Irish-speakers had only a rudimentary knowledge of the language gained in school or in Gaelic League classes.[17]

According to Adams, there were three types of Irish at that time: 1) Survival Irish, 2) Immigration Irish, 3) Revival Irish.

> The census figures as such make no distinction between survival Irish and the two types of rediffusion Irish – immigration and revivalist – so the dialectologist, for whom the first is important, the second of more limited interest, and the third a source of distortion in the records, must make allowances in interpreting distribution maps for different possibilities according to the nature of the area and the likelihood of immigration or revivalism affecting the picture.[18]

There seems little doubt but that it is *Survival Irish* which is of paramount importance in the district under study here. There is no evidence that there was any improvement in the status of Irish in this remote area of Beara prior to 1911 and it is my opinion that *Revival Irish* had little if any impact on the figures until the 1926 census. Indeed, the shame and embarrassment of the people about their ability to speak Irish was very obvious to Peadar Ó hAnnracháin, as mentioned above. It is my opinion, therefore that when people said in 1901 and 1911 that they or their children could speak Irish that they were giving a very honest opinion and that *Survival Irish* was the norm.

On the contrary, it is about the people who denied knowledge of Irish that we should have the greatest doubts, especially in the case of the 1901 census. For example, there was one family in Kilcatherine in 1901 in which nobody was recorded as having Irish. Among these was a widow of sixty years of age and a man of thirty.[19] This is almost impossible to believe because there was only one other person over twenty in Kilcatherine, between the censuses of 1901 and 1911, who admitted to having no Irish (a man of twenty-four years of age). As regards *Immigration Irish* there is simply no evidence from the census return forms that immigrants could have had any effect, either positive or negative, on the number of Irish speakers in this district as very few people – apart from a few servants and a small number of people from Co. Kerry who married into the area – were moving into the parish. Most of these people were simply Irish speakers moving into households in which all the adults were Irish-speaking themselves.

It is very important to mention here that there were only two children under ten years of age (one three year old from Kilcatherine[20] and an eight year old from Inward Ardgroom[21] – both 1901) from the whole parish of Kilcatherine during the taking of the 1901 and 1911 censuses who were recorded as monoglot Irish speakers. All the other monoglot Irish speakers were of the older generation. It is of interest also that most of these people were women (87 women and 21 men in 1901 and 35 women and 16 men in 1911). Possibly one of the reasons for this was that women tended to be much more confined to the home and that the men frequently went far beyond the parish boundary on fishing trips or as migratory labourers, and therefore had many more opportunities to mix with English speakers.

Another very important finding from the study of the census forms was the widespread occurrence of change in language in the middle of families. This was seen in 132 families in 1901 and in 97 in 1911. Following are samples of four families from this parish in which this phenomenon is clearly seen:

TABLE 2.

| Census Year | Townland | Age Children Irish & English | Age Children English only |
|---|---|---|---|
| Family 1. 1901 | Barrs | 19, 12, 12 | 10, 8, 6, 4, 2, 1[22] |
| Family 2. 1901 | Barrs | 20, 14, 10 | 9, 7, 5, 3[23] |
| Family 3. 1911 | Kilcatherine | 12, 11 | 9, 7, 5, 3[24] |
| Family 4. 1911 | Outward Ardgroom | 27, 24, 20, | 18, 16, 15 13, 11, 10, 8[25] |

There could be any one of three reasons for these cases:

1. The parents, having spoken Irish to the older children, to have consciously turned to English with the younger children or with the whole family.

2. English having been spoken to the children from the beginning, Irish being picked up outside the household by the older children, as had been happening frequently in the Gaeltacht until recently.

3. Irish having been learned in the home from grandparents or other older relatives by the older children. One man from Kilcatherine told me that he spoke fluent Irish as a child because his grandmother had no English. Indeed, his parents spoke no Irish to the children although they themselves spoke it fluently. This man had almost completely lost his ability to converse in Irish when I met him as an old man although his understanding of it was very good.[26]

The census return forms from Peig Minihane's own family for 1901 and 1911 may help to throw some light on what the linguistic situation was in that and other households in Beara and indeed in other parts of rural Ireland around that time. I have summarised the relevant parts of these forms for the two censuses in Table 3. It is interesting to note that the first six children are recorded in 1901 as being able to speak Irish and English, with the other three – Johanna (5), Mike (3) and Ellie (2) – recorded as having English only. It would seem that English must have been the language spoken to these younger children but we cannot be certain that Irish was spoken to the older ones. It is important to remember that Peig's father-in-law was in the house when she first married and it is probable that Irish was still regularly spoken in the house at that time. It was probably quite common at that time for the speaking of Irish in a household to end with the death of a grandparent and many children may have picked up the language passively in this way.

On the other hand, when we look at the situation in 1911 we see that Johanna (17) and Mike (15) are now recorded as being able to speak Irish and English with the four younger children having English only. What was the cause of this change in the ability of Johanna and Mike to speak Irish and why were Ellie (13), Eugene (11), Peter (10) and Tim (8) unable to speak it? Did Johanna and Mike pick up Irish in their own home or from other children? However the children in this household acquired the language we can have little doubt but that this census form gives an honest assessment of the perceived linguistic ability of the different members of the family especially when we note that although Jerry and Mary were now in America and should not have been included they were still recorded on the form as having both Irish and English, their names being later crossed out, probably by the enumerator. However we still do not know what degree of proficiency in Irish any of these children had and we can be fairly certain that most of them did not have the fluency of their parents:

> So, after the Famine, English began to be introduced to such an extent into the home and neighbourhood domains in most Irish-speaking communities that the children became primarily English-speaking and, at most, acquired a passive competence in Irish. The diglossic pattern, which though progressively weakened, had maintained the Irish language through a century and a half of fairly widespread bilingualism, was finally breaking down and, over a large part of the country, a rapid language shift began to take place.[27]

However, in the case of Peig Minihane's children we do know that Mike retained his ability to speak Irish throughout his life, that he had a great regard for the language, and that he taught it to fellow prisoners on Spike Island when he and his brother Eugene spent some time there during the Civil War.[28] It may of course be that the nationalist ideology of the time influenced him to take a special interest in the language of his parents and to strengthen and consolidate his knowledge of it.

Table 8 shows a more complete picture of the distribution of this type of family bilingualism throughout all the townlands of Kilcatherine Parish. Although it is clear that these matters are somewhat complex, whatever caused this difference in the ability of children in the same family to speak Irish, it was a widespread phenomenon, and seems to me to be the most ominous sign of a radical change in people's attitude to the language and of the disaster that was to befall it in the coming years.

TABLE 3

*Irish speaking in the O'Sullivan family, Gurteen*

| Name | DoB | 1901 Census | 1911 Census |
|------|-----|-------------|-------------|
| Mary | b.1884 | Ir/Eng | Ir/Eng |
| Dan | b.1885 | Ir/Eng | Died in Butte, Montana |
| Jerry | b.1887 | Ir/Eng | Ir/Eng |
| John | b.1888 | Ir/Eng | Died aged 16 |
| Patrick | b.1891 | Ir/Eng | Ir/Eng |
| Margaret | b.1893 | Ir/Eng | Ir/Eng |
| Johanna | b.1894 | Eng | Ir/Eng |
| Mike | b.1896 | Eng | Ir/Eng |
| Ellie | b.1897 | Eng | Eng |
| Brigid | b.1899 | Died Young | |
| Eugene | b.1901 | | Eng |
| Peter | b.1902 | | Eng |
| Tim | b.1903 | | Eng |

TABLE 4

*Irish Speakers in Barony of Bear & Castletown Rural District*

Barony of Bear

| Census | Irish Only | No. Irish Speakers | % Irish Speakers |
|--------|-----------|--------------------|-----------------|
| 1851 | 4,278 | 11,811 | 59.3 |
| 1861 | 3,054 | 12,247 | 74.2 |
| 1871 | 2,147 | 9,974 | 63.1 |
| 1881 | 949 | 9,564 | 62.7 |
| 1891 | 531 | 7,183 | 51.5 |

Castletown Rural District[29]

| Census | Irish Only | No. Irish Speakers | % Irish Speakers |
|--------|-----------|--------------------|-----------------|
| 1901 | 193 | 5,774 | 51.7 |
| 1911 | 86 | 5,160 | 49.6 |
| 1926 | 12 | 4,122 | 44.0 |
| 1936 | – | 4,050 | 54.5 |
| 1946 | – | 3,125 | 49.3 |

TABLE 5

*The Population of Kilcatherine Parish*

| Townland | 1841 | 1851 | 1861 | 1871 | 1881 | 1891 | 1901 | 1911 |
|---|---|---|---|---|---|---|---|---|
| Ahabrock | 121 | 88 | 61 | 34 | 50 | 66 | 65 | 48 |
| Ardacluggan | 92 | 72 | 70 | 57 | 66 | 55 | 63 | 68 |
| Inward Ardgroom | 802 | 491 | 425 | 387 | 388 | 322 | 254 | 252 |
| Outward Ardgroom | 790 | 533 | 512 | 519 | 516 | 438 | 405 | 391 |
| Ballycrovane | 156 | 110 | 160 | 157 | 125[30] | 234[31] | 108[32] | 61 |
| Barrs | 68 | 53 | 42 | 41 | 48 | 47 | 52 | 28 |
| Bawnard | 46 | 27 | 29 | 24 | 21 | 20 | 14 | 13 |
| Boffickil | 179 | 85 | 103 | 73 | 71 | 55 | 49 | 46 |
| Bunskellig | 61 | 33 | 37 | 31 | 47 | 28 | 23 | 26 |
| Cahiravart | 48 | 11 | 8 | 14 | 15 | 9 | 14 | 24 |
| Cahirkeem | 513 | 414 | 312 | 269 | 247 | 214 | 195 | 179 |
| Carrig | 43 | 23 | 23 | 29 | 33 | 35 | 29 | 20 |
| Clogher | 8 | 0 | 0 | 0 | 0 | 0 | 0 | 0 |
| Clountreem | 36 | 30 | 32 | 35 | 32 | 26 | 32 | 20 |
| Commons East | 6 | 0 | 0 | 9 | 5 | 8 | 7 | 4 |
| Commons West | 51 | 0 | 0 | 0 | 0 | 0 | 0 | 0 |
| Coulagh | 413 | 252 | 242 | 227 | 208 | 155 | 144 | 117 |
| Croumhane | 285 | 249 | 191 | 172 | 183 | 171 | 148 | 146 |
| Eyeries | 394 | 274 | 252 | 238 | 168 | 192 | 183 | 176 |
| Eyeries Town | 222 | 217 | 140 | 137 | 150 | 140 | 135 | 149 |
| Faunkill & the Woods | 123 | 116 | 32 | 45 | 92 | 93 | 78 | 57 |
| Glenbeg | 60 | 16 | 34 | 42 | 45 | 42 | 39 | 32 |
| Gortatornora | 13 | 16 | 18 | 16 | 22 | 18 | 13 | 14 |
| Gortgariff | 317 | 149 | 145 | 132 | 143 | 100 | 76 | 93 |
| Gowlane | 61 | 62 | 78 | 84 | 82 | 53 | 46 | 49 |
| Inches | 388 | 240 | 219 | 205 | 220 | 202 | 160 | 153 |
| Inchinteskin | 83 | 84 | 70 | 80 | 79 | 84 | 71 | 55 |
| Inisfarnard | 30 | 28 | 35 | 35 | 26 | 24 | 25 | 11 |
| Kilcatherine | 821 | 521 | 486 | 441 | 431 | 400 | 371 | 349 |
| Kilmackowen | 146 | 128 | 105 | 121 | 136 | 128 | 135 | 127 |
| Urhan | 564 | 257 | 264 | 256 | 275 | 244 | 235 | 214 |
| **Total** | **6,940** | **4,579** | **4,125** | **3,910** | **3,924** | **3,603** | **3,169** | **2,922** |

## TABLE 6
*Irish Speakers in Townlands of Kilcatherine Parish, 1901 Census*

| Townland | Irish only | | No. | % | Age Ir-Speaking Children | | | | |
|---|---|---|---|---|---|---|---|---|---|
| | M | F | Speakers | Speakers | 0–2 | 3–4 | 5–9 | 10–14 | 15–20 |
| Ahabrock | 0 | 1 | 46 | 70.7 | 0 | 0 | 1 | 1 | 7 |
| Ardacluggan | 0 | 0 | 41 | 65.1 | 0 | 0 | 2 | 3 | 5 |
| Inward Ardgroom | 5 | 13 | 206 | 81.1 | 2 | 0 | 13 | 25 | 39 |
| Outward Ardgroom | 3 | 9 | 231 | 74.0 | 0 | 1 | 22 | 47 | 46 |
| Ardgroom Town | 1 | 2 | 54 | 58.1 | 0 | 0 | 2 | 2 | 10 |
| Ballycrovane | 1 | 1 | 69 | 92.0 | 0 | 1 | 9 | 10 | 15 |
| Barrs | 0 | 0 | 36 | 69.2 | 0 | 0 | 5 | 7 | 7 |
| Bawnard | 0 | 0 | 14 | 100.0 | 0 | 1 | 1 | 5 | 2 |
| Boffickil | 0 | 1 | 44 | 89.8 | 0 | 1 | 5 | 3 | 13 |
| Bunskellig | 0 | 0 | 9 | 39.1 | 0 | 0 | 0 | 0 | 0 |
| Cahiravart | 0 | 0 | 9 | 64.3 | 0 | 0 | 0 | 0 | 0 |
| Cahirkeem | 0 | 9 | 140 | 71.8 | 0 | 0 | 11 | 21 | 25 |
| Carrig | 0 | 0 | 21 | 72.4 | 0 | 0 | 0 | 2 | 9 |
| Clogher | 0 | 0 | 0 | 00.0 | 0 | 0 | 0 | 0 | 0 |
| Clountreem | 0 | 0 | 12 | 37.5 | 0 | 0 | 0 | 0 | 0 |
| Commons East | 0 | 0 | 2 | 28.6 | 0 | 0 | 0 | 0 | 0 |
| Commons West | 0 | 0 | 0 | 00.0 | 0 | 0 | 0 | 0 | 0 |
| Coulagh | 0 | 5 | 102 | 70.8 | 0 | 0 | 5 | 12 | 24 |
| Croumhane | 0 | 2 | 92 | 62.2 | 0 | 0 | 5 | 7 | 17 |
| Eyeries | 1 | 2 | 112 | 61.2 | 0 | 1 | 3 | 16 | 21 |
| Eyeries Town | 0 | 1 | 99 | 73.3 | 0 | 0 | 3 | 14 | 16 |
| Faunkill & Woods | 0 | 2 | 48 | 61.5 | 0 | 1 | 5 | 7 | 10 |
| Glenbeg | 0 | 0 | 28 | 71.8 | 0 | 0 | 4 | 3 | 5 |
| Gortatornora | 0 | 1 | 13 | 100.0 | 0 | 0 | 0 | 2 | 3 |
| Gortgariff | 3 | 5 | 68 | 89.5 | 0 | 1 | 4 | 7 | 10 |
| Gowlane | 0 | 0 | 41 | 89.1 | 0 | 0 | 0 | 3 | 11 |
| Inches | 0 | 4 | 117 | 73.1 | 0 | 0 | 1 | 12 | 31 |
| Inchinteskin | 0 | 1 | 66 | 93.0 | 0 | 1 | 6 | 9 | 14 |
| Inisfarnard | 7 | 4 | 23 | 92.0 | 0 | 0 | 3 | 4 | 5 |
| Kilcatherine | 8 | 21 | 299 | 80.6 | 0 | 5 | 36 | 38 | 56 |
| Kilmackowen | 0 | 0 | 108 | 80.0 | 1 | 2 | 12 | 19 | 17 |
| Urhan | 0 | 1 | 132 | 56.2 | 0 | 0 | 4 | 12 | 20 |
| **Total** | **29** | **85** | **2282** | **72.8** | **3** | **15** | **162** | **291** | **438** |

TABLE 7

*Irish Speakers in Townlands of Kilcatherine Parish, 1911 Census*

| Townland | Irish only | | No. Speakers | % Speakers | Age Ir-Speaking Children | | | | |
|---|---|---|---|---|---|---|---|---|---|
| | M | F | | | 0–2 | 3–4 | 5–9 | 10–14 | 15–20 |
| Ahabrock | 0 | 0 | 34 | 70.8 | 0 | 0 | 1 | 8 | 8 |
| Ardacluggan | 0 | 2 | 38 | 55.9 | 0 | 1 | 2 | 4 | 3 |
| Inward Ardgroom | 1 | 3 | 176 | 69.8 | 3 | 5 | 15 | 18 | 20 |
| Outward Ardgroom | 0 | 0 | 200 | 64.7 | 2 | 1 | 8 | 28 | 33 |
| Ardgroom Town | 0 | 1 | 44 | 53.7 | 0 | 0 | 2 | 4 | 7 |
| Ballycrovane | 1 | 2 | 46 | 75.4 | 0 | 0 | 1 | 1 | 4 |
| Barrs | 0 | 1 | 15 | 53.6 | 0 | 0 | 0 | 3 | 2 |
| Bawnard | 0 | 0 | 11 | 84.6 | 0 | 0 | 0 | 0 | 1 |
| Boffickil | 0 | 0 | 31 | 67.4 | 0 | 0 | 1 | 2 | 4 |
| Bunskellig | 0 | 0 | 10 | 38.5 | 0 | 0 | 0 | 0 | 0 |
| Cahiravart | 0 | 0 | 6 | 25.0 | 0 | 0 | 0 | 2 | 1 |
| Cahirkeem | 0 | 4 | 107 | 59.8 | 0 | 0 | 4 | 16 | 18 |
| Carrig | 0 | 0 | 17 | 85.0 | 0 | 0 | 1 | 2 | 0 |
| Clogher | 0 | 0 | 0 | 00.0 | 0 | 0 | 0 | 0 | 0 |
| Clountreem | 0 | 0 | 12 | 60.0 | 0 | 0 | 0 | 11 | 3 |
| Commons East | 0 | 0 | 1 | 25.0 | 0 | 0 | 0 | 0 | 0 |
| Commons West | 0 | 0 | 0 | 00.0 | 0 | 0 | 0 | 0 | 0 |
| Coulagh | 0 | 1 | 61 | 52.1 | 0 | 0 | 1 | 8 | 13 |
| Croumhane | 1 | 1 | 78 | 53.4 | 0 | 0 | 4 | 12 | 6 |
| Eyeries | 1 | 0 | 87 | 49.4 | 0 | 1 | 6 | 7 | 8 |
| Eyeries Town | 0 | 2 | 75 | 50.3 | 0 | 0 | 3 | 2 | 9 |
| Faunkill & Woods | 0 | 0 | 34 | 59.6 | 0 | 1 | 0 | 7 | 6 |
| Glenbeg | 0 | 1 | 20 | 62.5 | 1 | 0 | 2 | 4 | 2 |
| Gortatornora | 0 | 0 | 9 | 64.3 | 0 | 0 | 0 | 0 | 0 |
| Gowlane | 0 | 2 | 21 | 42.9 | 0 | 0 | 0 | 0 | 0 |
| Inches | 1 | 2 | 79 | 51.6 | 0 | 0 | 1 | 8 | 8 |
| Inchinteskin | 0 | 2 | 40 | 72.7 | 0 | 0 | 2 | 2 | 9 |
| Kilcatherine | 7 | 8 | 268 | 76.8 | 2 | 12 | 31 | 40 | 39 |
| Gortgariff | 4 | 2 | 77 | 82.8 | 1 | 4 | 13 | 10 | 6 |
| Kilmackowen | 0 | 0 | 71 | 55.9 | 0 | 0 | 3 | 10 | 10 |
| Urhan | 0 | 0 | 122 | 57.0 | 0 | 0 | 3 | 16 | 29 |
| Inisfarnard | 0 | 1 | 10 | 90.9 | 0 | 0 | 0 | 0 | 4 |
| **Total** | **16** | **35** | **1800** | **61.6** | **9** | **25** | **104** | **225** | **253** |

TABLE 8

*Irish-speaking Households in Townlands of Kilcatherine Parish: 1901 & 1911*
ISC in H = Irish-Speaking Children in Household

| Townland | Census | No ISC in H | Some ISC in H | All ISC in H |
|---|---|---|---|---|
| Ardacluggan | 1901 | 3 | 3 | 1 |
| | 1911 | 5 | 3 | 0 |
| Inward Ardgroom | 1901 | 6 | 7 | 21 |
| | 1911 | 13 | 10 | 11 |
| Outward Ardgroom | 1901 | 14 | 14 | 18 |
| | 1911 | 14 | 8 | 16 |
| Ardgroom Town | 1901 | 6 | 3 | 3 |
| | 1911 | 3 | 4 | 3 |
| Ahabrock | 1901 | 4 | 2 | 1 |
| | 1911 | 0 | 2 | 3 |

| | | | | |
|---|---|---|---|---|
| Ballycrovane | 1901 | 0 | 2 | 10 |
| | 1911 | 2 | 2 | 1 |
| Barrs | 1901 | 0 | 4 | 0 |
| | 1911 | 3 | 1 | 1 |
| Bawnard | 1901 | 0 | 0 | 2 |
| | 1911 | 1 | 0 | 1 |
| Boffickil | 1901 | 0 | 2 | 3 |
| | 1911 | 3 | 1 | 1 |
| Bunskellig | 1901 | 4 | 0 | 0 |
| | 1911 | 4 | 0 | 0 |
| Cahiravart | 1901 | 2 | 0 | 0 |
| | 1911 | 1 | 1 | 0 |
| Cahirkeem | 1901 | 2 | 11 | 11 |
| | 1911 | 7 | 7 | 5 |
| Carrig | 1901 | 0 | 2 | 2 |
| | 1911 | 2 | 0 | 1 |
| Clogher | 1901 | 0 | 0 | 0 |
| | 1911 | 0 | 0 | 0 |
| Clountreem | 1901 | 4 | 0 | 0 |
| | 1911 | 1 | 1 | 0 |
| Commons East | 1901 | 1 | 0 | 0 |
| | 1911 | 1 | 0 | 0 |
| Commons West | 1901 | 0 | 0 | 0 |
| | 1911 | 0 | 0 | 0 |
| Coulagh | 1901 | 3 | 8 | 9 |
| | 1911 | 9 | 3 | 2 |
| Croumhane | 1901 | 10 | 5 | 7 |
| | 1911 | 8 | 5 | 4 |
| Eyeries | 1901 | 12 | 6 | 9 |
| | 1911 | 12 | 4 | 5 |
| Eyeries Town | 1901 | 1 | 9 | 2 |
| | 1911 | 11 | 3 | 4 |
| Faunkill & The Woods | 1901 | 1 | 5 | 2 |
| | 1911 | 3 | 3 | 0 |
| Glenbeg | 1901 | 3 | 2 | 1 |
| | 1911 | 3 | 2 | 1 |
| Gortornora | 1901 | 0 | 0 | 2 |
| | 1911 | 2 | 0 | 0 |
| Gowlane | 1901 | 1 | 1 | 6 |
| | 1911 | 7 | 0 | 0 |
| Inches | 1901 | 5 | 10 | 6 |
| | 1911 | 10 | 4 | 4 |
| Inchinteskin | 1901 | 0 | 3 | 5 |
| | 1911 | 3 | 2 | 3 |
| Kilcatherine | 1901 | 7 | 15 | 23 |
| | 1911 | 6 | 13 | 23 |
| Gortgariff | 1901 | 1 | 2 | 8 |
| | 1911 | 1 | 4 | 8 |
| Kilmackowen | 1901 | 3 | 3 | 10 |
| | 1911 | 8 | 4 | 5 |
| Urhan | 1901 | 11 | 12 | 2 |
| | 1911 | 10 | 9 | 6 |
| Inisfarnard | 1901 | 0 | 1 | 2 |
| | 1911 | 0 | 1 | 0 |
| **Total** | **1901** | **104** | **132** | **166** |
| | **1911** | **153** | **97** | **108** |

1 G. FitzGerald, 'Estimates for Baronies of Minimum Level of Irish-Speaking amongst Successive Decennial Cohorts: 1771–1781 to 1861–1871', *Proceedings of the Royal Academy*, 84 C (1984), No. 3.

2 F. Roper, Parliamentary Papers – Report of the Commissioners, p. 866.

3 B. Ó Cuív, *Irish Dialects and Irish-Speaking Districts* (Baile Átha Cliath: Institiúid Ard-Léinn Bhaile Átha Cliath, 1971), p. 20.

4 D. Cowman, 'Life and Labour in Three Irish Mining Communities circa 1840', *Saothar: Iris an Chumainn le Stair Lucht Saothair na hÉireann*, 9 (1983), p. 18.

5 O'Dwyer, *Who Were My Ancestors – Genealogy (Family Trees) of the Eyeries Parish, Castletownbere, Co. Cork, Ireland* (Astoria 3, USA: Stevens Publishing Co. 1976), p. 101

6 David M. Emmons, *The Butte Irish – Class and Ethnicity in an American Mining Town, 1875–1925* (1993), p. 15.

7 IFC Vol. 1224:276.

8 *Ibid.*, p. 277.

9 An account of her memories of her grandmother written for me in longhand by Noreen Heaney (O'Sullivan), Glasnevin, Dublin (who was born and reared in Gurteen, Ardgroom, Co. Cork), Christmas, 1991.

10 The National Archives, Dublin: Census of Ireland, 1901, Cork 42/17, p. 7 (Gortgarriff).

11 Noreen Heaney's account.

12 P. Ó hAnnracháin, *Fé Bhrat an Chonnartha* (Baile Átha Cliath, Oifig an tSoláthair, 1944), p. 214.

13 *Ibid.*, p. 213

14 *Ibid.*

15 IFC Vol. 637:141.

16 B. Ní Mhóráin, *Thiar sa Mhainistir Atá an Ghaolainn Bhreá* (An Daingean: An Sagart, 1997), pp. 147–54.

17 G. B. Adams, 'The Validity of Language Census Figures', *Ulster Folklife*, 25 (1979), p. 116.

18 G. B. Adams, 'The Last Language Census in Northern Ireland', *Ulster Dialects* (Hollywood, Ulster Folk Museum, 1964), p. 114.

19 The National Archives, Dublin: Census of Ireland, 1901, Cork, 42/19, 44 (Kilcatherine).

20 The National Archives, Dublin: Census of Ireland, 1901, Cork, 42/19, 58 (Kilcatherine).

21 The National Archives, Dublin: Census of Ireland, 1901, Cork, 42/1, 1 (Inward Ardgroom).

22 The National Archives, Dublin: Census of Ireland, 1901, Cork, 42/2, 30 (Outward Ardgroom).

23 The National Archives, Dublin: Census of Ireland, 1901, Cork, 42/4, 3 (Barees).

24 The National Archives, Dublin: Census of Ireland, 1911, Cork, 42/19, 25 (Kilcatherine).

25 The National Archives, Dublin: Census of Ireland, 1911, Cork, 42/2, 30 (Outward Ardgroom).

26 A personal interview with Quinlan O'Sullivan, Tuairín Bán na Gréine, Kilcatherine.

27 M. Ó Murchú, *Language and Community* (Dublin: Government Publications, 1970), p. 28.

28 Mike's daughter, Noreen Heaney, sent me some extracts from an autograph book which her father brought home from Spike Island. In one extract, dated 29/8/21, P. Lynch, NT, of Aherlow, Co. Tipperary is quoted:

> Dear Micheál, we shall never forget you
> For the kindness you've shown unto us,
> In teaching us the tongue of our fathers,
> Amidst all the hurry and fuss.

29 1891 was the last year in which the Barony was used as a unit in the Census of Ireland. The Rural District was then brought into use which was further divided into District Electoral Divisions. Glengarriff and Kilcaskan District Electoral Divisions were now included in Bantry Rural.

30 Some of the houses which had been included in Ballycrovane in 1871 were included in Faunkill and the Woods for this census.

31 141 people on board ship are included here.

32 33 people on board ship are included here.

TABLE 1 IS BASED ON DATA EXTRACTED FROM:
G. FitzGerald, 'Estimates for Baronies of Minimum Level of Irish-Speaking amongst Successive Decennial Cohorts: 1771–1781 to 1861–1871', *Proceedings of the Royal Academy*, 84 C (1984), No. 3, p. 132.

TABLE 2 IS BASED ON THE FOLLOWING SOURCES:
The National Archives, Dublin: Census of Ireland, 1901, Cork 42/4, 4 (Barees).
The National Archives, Dublin: Census of Ireland, 1901, Cork 42/4, 3 (Barees).
The National Archives, Dublin: Census of Ireland, 1911, Cork 42/19, 25 (Kilcatherine).
The National Archives, Dublin: Census of Ireland, 1911, Cork 42/4, 30 (Outward Ardgroom).

TABLE 3 IS BASED ON THE FOLLOWING SOURCES:
The National Archives, Dublin: Census of Ireland, 1901, Cork 42/2, 30 (Outward Ardgroom).
The National Archives, Dublin: Census of Ireland, 1911, Cork 42/2, 30 (Outward Ardgroom).

TABLE 4 IS BASED ON THE FOLLOWING SOURCES:
*Census Report, 1851, Education of the People, Cork W. Riding*, p. 268.
*Census Report, 1861, Education of the People, Munster*, p. 1006–7.
*Census Report, 1871, Education of the People, County and City of Cork*, p. 395.
*Census Report, 1891, Education of the People, County and City of Cork*, p. 395.
*Census Report, 1901, Education of the People, County and City of Cork*, p. 385
*Census Report, 1911, Education of the People, County and City of Cork*, p. 354–355.
*Census Report, 1926*, Vol. 8, p. 14.
*Census Report, 1936*, Vol. 8, p. 14.
*Census Report, 1946*, Vol. 8, p. 14.

TABLE 5 IS BASED ON THE FOLLOWING SOURCES:
*Census Report, 1841*, Addenda, Cork West Riding, p. 5–6.
*Census Report, 1851*, Part 1, Vol. 2, Munster, p. 123–24.
*Census Report, 1861*, Part 1, Vol. 2, Munster, p. 123–24.
*Census Report, 1871*, Part 1, Vol. 2, Munster, p. 219–20.
*Census Report, 1881*, Part 1, Vol. 2, Munster, p. 219–20.
*Census Report, 1891*, Part 1, Vol. 2, Munster, p. 219–20.
*Census Report, 1901*, Part 1, Vol. 2, City and County of Cork, p. 28–30.
*Census Report, 1911*, Part 1, City and County of Cork, p. 27–30.

TABLES 6, 7 AND 8 ARE BASED ON THE FOLLOWING SOURCES:
The National Archives, Dublin: Census of Ireland, 1901 & 1911, Cork, for the following townlands: Clontreen, Gowlane, Kilmackowen, Ardacluggin, Aughabrack, Cahirkeem, Coulagh, Inchinteskin, Urhin, Inward Ardgroom, Outward Ardgroom, Ballycrovane, Barees, Bawnard, Bofickil, Bunskellig, Caheravart, Carrig, Clogher, Commons East, Crumpane, Eyeries, Faunkill and The Woods, Glenbeg, Gortatornora, Gortgarriff, Inches, Kilcatherine, Inisfarnard, Eyeries Town, Ardgroom Town.

EDITORIAL NOTES

**Local Lore (pp. 11–15)**

LOCAL SETTLERS AND INHABITANTS

Coastguards in Ballycrovane – 24/9/51: IFC Vol. 1224:306–7. According to the 1901 Census of Ireland there were three families of coastguards in Ballycrovane: Thompson, Lloyd and Nunny. George Thompson was from Portsmouth and his wife Lucy was from Dorset; they had three children (The National Archives, Dublin: Census of Ireland, 1901, Cork, 42/13 (Eyeries)/15). William Lloyd was a Protestant Episcopalian and his wife Elizabeth was a Catholic. They were both English and they had two children (The National Archives, Dublin: Census of Ireland, 1901, Cork, 42/13 (Eyeries)/16). William Nunny was Welsh and his wife Mary was from Co. Dublin. They were both Catholics and, according to the 1901 Census returns, Mary could speak both Irish and English (The National Archives, Dublin: Census of Ireland, 1901, Cork, 42/13 (Eyeries)/17). For lore regarding the large number of people living in Kilcatherine Point before the Famine see IFC Vol. 1224:330–32, collected by Tadhg Ó Murchú from Pádraig Ó Laochdha, Kilcatherine, 17/9/51.

MIDDLEMEN AND LANDLORDS

Máire Ní Ghearail' and Mac Finín Duibh – 11/9/51: IFC Vol. 1224:178–81. Mac Finín Duibh's residence was in Dereen in the parish of Tuosist in Co. Kerr, (S. Ó Súilleabháin, *Diarmaid Ó na Bolgaighe agus a Chomharsain* (Baile Átha Cliath: Muintir Chathail, Clódóirí, 1937), p. 179). The Mac Finín Duibh family belonged to the O'Sullivan Bere clan who were the old Gaelic landlords of the area (W. F. T. Butler, *Gleanings From Irish History* (London, Green and Co., 1925), p. 34). The last Mac Finín Duibh was born in 1756. His name was Sylvester Mac Finín Duibh and his servant found him dead on the road after he had fallen from his horse on the way home from Co. Limerick (Ó Súilleabháin, *Diarmaid na Bolgaighe*, p. 181). His body was brought home to Tuosist and it was said that the crowd attending his funeral was the largest ever seen in Tuosist (Ó Súilleabháin, *Diarmaid na Bolgaighe*, p. 182). For further information about this family see Lyne (1975), G. Lyne, 'The Mac Finín Duibh O'Sullivans of Tuosist and Bearhaven', JKAHS 9 (1976): 32–67. For other examples of the traditional view of landlords and middlemen in Beara see IFC Vol. 623:384–86, 389–92; 1188:202–7; 1224:23–33, 313–14, 314–21, 322–25.

THE FAMINE

1. Graves by the ditchside during the Famine – 14/7/50: IFC Vol. 1188:256–57. Pádraig Ó Sé of Gort a' Leasa told of a Famine grave marked by a standing stone which he was informed about by his uncle when he was in Springfield, USA, IFC Vol. 1188:351–52. Pádraig Ó Laochdha, Kilcatherine also spoke to Tadhg Ó Murchú of Famine graves by the roadside, e.g., one in Droinn a' Chuais and another east of Kilcatherine school, IFC Vol. 1224:325–26. The same informant also described the death of two neighbour's children from hunger, as witnessed by his own mother, IFC Vol. 1224:326–27. Pádraig also mentioned the seeming relief of a widow from Cuailleach at the death of her child when, having wrapped it in some clothes and buried it, she exclaims: *'Baochais le Dia nách é an bia a chuireas!'* ['Thanks be to God that it wasn't the food I buried!'] This anecdote graphically illustrates the anguish and loss of all normal emotions which may be experienced

by people in the face of extreme hunger and deprivation, IFC Vol. 1224:327–28. It is interesting that almost identical words were attributed to a woman from near Dunquin, Co. Kerry in an item collected from Peig Sayers. The woman, having carried her sixteen year old daughter to the graveyard and buried her, is quoted by Peig as having said to a neighbour who gave her potatoes to eat on her way home: *'Mhuise buíochas mór le Dia mar phráta ... nách tú a chuireas i mBaile na hAbha anois'* ['wisha thanks be to God to you for a potato ... that it wasn't you I buried in Baile na hAbha today'], IFC Vol. 1070:12–14. Donncha Ó Rócháin of Droinn na mBéilleac spoke [10/5/39] of a man called Féidhlim Mac Cárthaigh who died in Droinn a' Chuais but whose body was too heavy to carry across the hill to Kilcatherine graveyard. He was buried in a field. Donncha also mentioned a woman who is buried in a little field in Tuairín Bán, IFC Vol. 623:322–23. Diarmaid Ó hUrdail [Diarmaid Caobach] of Kilcatherine told [3/5/39] of a woman whose body was rooted up by pigs during the Famine and whose child had to be subsequently placed in Kenmare Workhouse. Her grieving husband went wandering the world but later returned home and married again, IFC Vol. 623:180–82. Diarmaid Ó Sé of Fán Shliabh described [10/9/51] the death of two little girls in a field on the mountainside as told to him by his father-in-law. One of the girls had the flesh eaten from her fingers, IFC Vol. 1224:21–22. For other references to the death of children in Beara during the Famine see IFC Vol. 623: 177–78; 1224:21.

2. The picking of white periwinkles during the Famine (i) – 14/7/50: IFC Vol. 1188: 256.

3. The picking of white periwinkles during the Famine (ii) – 25/7/50: IFC Vol. 1188: 267. It is not quite clear what species of mollusc is being referred to here by the informant. She uses the Irish word *piachán* in one instance and *préachán* in another. Although *faocha* is the standard Irish word, *piachán* is used in parts of Munster for periwinkle and it is most likely that 'black periwinkle' is used here for 'edible periwinkle' *[Littorina littorea]* and 'white periwinkle' for one of the other species of *Littorina* [flat, rough or small periwinkle]. For another reference from Beara to the eating of shellfish during the Famine see IFC Vol. 623:182–83.

4. Eating charlock during the Famine – 14/7/50: IFC Vol. 1188:257. Charlock *(Sinapsis arvensis) (Praiseach Bhuí)* was sold on the streets of Dublin as a vegetable during the eighteenth century (N. Williams, *Díolaim Luibheanna* (Dublin: Sáirséal Ó Marcaigh, 1993), p. 142). Patricia Lysaght has discussed its use as a Famine food as well as the role of women as producers and procurers of food during the Famine, (See P. Lysaght, 'Women During the Great Irish Famine', *Béaloideas*, 64–65, 1996–1997), pp. 77–90). See also A. T. Lucus' discussion of the use of nettles and charlock as Famine food, 'Nettles and Charlock as Famine Food,' *Breifne 2* (1959), pp. 137–46.

5. Watching the garden during the Famine (i) – 14/7/50: IFC Vol. 1188:256. Cormac Ó Gráda has briefly discussed this tradition that stealing occurred during the Famine and points out that names of people involved were seldom mentioned in accounts of this nature (C. Ó Gráda, *An Drochshaol – Béaloideas agus Amhráin* (Coiscéim, Baile Átha Cliath, 1994), p. 17–19).

6. Watching the garden during the Famine (ii) – 25/7/50: IFC Vol. 1188:267.

7. Eating seaweed – 14/7/50: IFC Vol. 1188:257.

8. Working on the roads during the Famine – 25/7/50: IFC Vol. 1188:267–68. Pádraig Ó Sé of Gort a' Leasa told [25/7/50] of how his grandfather and two of his uncles worked on the 'Board of Works Road' during the Famine, IFC Vol. 1188:350–51.

9. Spike – 14/7/50: IFC Vol. 1188:253–56. Another version of this story was collected

by Eoghan Ó Súilleabháin from Mícheál Ó Síocháin of Barra Coille [12/3/37], IFC Vol. 312:445–47.

## The Livelihood of the People (pp. 16–37)

WRECK AND SHORE GATHERING

1. Gathering wreck on the Point – 21/9/51: IFC Vol. 1224:280–81.
2. A boy who was drowned while after wreck – 21/9/51: IFC Vol. 1224:281.
3. Bad luck that follows wreck – 21/9/51: IFC Vol. 1224:282. Pádraig Ó Laochdha, Kilcatherine, spoke [1950] of the pursuit by the coastguards of a boatload of wreck being brought to Kenmare by men from Inisfarnard, Dept of Irish Folklore, University College Dublin. Tape M906c–M912a.
4. Live fish on Saint Patrick's Day – 13/9/51: IFC Vol. 1224:218–19. Pádraig Ó Laochdha, Kilcatherine described [17/9/51] how a woman called Máiréad Ní Mhairineáin was swept off the rocks by a wave and drowned while gathering *míobhán* [Pepper dulse] *[Laurencia pinnatifida]* in Inisfarnard Island, IFC Vol. 1224:329–30. He also gave the names and descriptions of various types of seaweed and some of their practical uses [25/9/51], IFC Vol. 1224:361–62, 366–67.

FISHING – GENERAL INFORMATION

Catching crabs – 4/9/52: IFC Vol. 1312:140. Very valuable information about practical aspects of fishing in Beara was collected by Tadhg Ó Murchú from Pádraig Ó Laochdha, Kilcatherine during 1950 and 1951, IFC Vol. 1224: 332–43, 345–46, 350–51, 354–55; Dept of Irish Folklore, University College Dublin. Tape M906c– M912a.

DROWNINGS AND SEA ADVENTURES

1. Two who were tragically drowned – 13/9/51: IFC Vol. 1224:213–15. The man who was drowned was Patrick Fenton, a boat builder from Cathair Caim. He was born in Caherdaniel, Co. Kerry. His father's name was Thomas Fenton. Patrick was married to Mary Fitzgerald from Caherdaniel. They were married in Eyeries and they had twelve children. The boy who was drowned with Patrick was Daniel O'Sullivan, a son of Michael O'Sullivan (Mike O' The Strand) and Mary O'Sullivan (Suaimhnis), The Strand, Cathair Caim. Patrick Fenton, his son Tade, and Daniel O'Sullivan went to Lauragh, Co. Kerry for a load of timber on 4 March 1924. There was a heavy snowfall when they were about to sail for home. Tade stayed in Kilmackiloge where he was working and Patrick and Daniel sailed for home. The boat was swamped and sank as they passed between Inisfarnard and Kilcatherine Point. Patrick Hanley later found the wreck of the boat near Claonach in Rinn Troisc, Allihies Parish but the bodies were never found (O'Dwyer, *Who Were My Ancestors – Eyeries*, p. 265, 268).
2. How a boat from Cróchán was lost – 9/9/51: IFC Vol. 1224:123–24
3. Micil of the Island – 25/7/50: IFC Vol. 1188:260–64. Seana-Mhicheál O'Sullivan [Micil an Oileáin (Micil of the Island)] was the first child to be born in Inisfarnard island during modern times. He was a son of Daniel O'Sullivan and Máire O'Leary. Micheál married Catherine (Rohane) McCarthy from Doire Mhór, Kilcatherine. He used to pilot coal boats from the northern side of Inisfarnard up the Kenmare River to Kenmare. Micheál and Catherine had six children in the island, the first of whom, Mary, was born in 1846 (O'Dwyer, *Who Were My Ancestors – Eyeries*, p. 81–82).
4. Drowned fishermen seen ashore – IFC Vol. 1224:125–26. See also M. Verling, *Gort*

*Broc – Scéalta agus Seanchas Ó Bhéarra* (Dublin: Coiscéim, 1996), p. 237– 39 for another reference from Beara to drowned fishermen being seen ashore. A number of items concerning the harshness of life at sea and various fishing adventures and incidents were collected by Tadhg Ó Murchú from Mícheál Ó Dúnaí, Kilcatherine [16/5/39], IFC Vol. 623:548–59; Pádraig Ó Laochdha, Kilcatherine [17/9/51], IFC Vol. 1224:343–45, 346–47; and Diarmaid Ó Sé, Fán Shliaibh [24/7/1950], IFC Vol. 1188:244–46, [17/9/51] IFC Vol. 1224:65–71, and [20/9/51], IFC Vol. 1224: 94–95.

FISHING – FISHING BELIEFS

1. Saying the rosary going into the seine boat – 24/9/51: IFC Vol. 1224:312.
2. A prohibition against putting a drowned person's body into the boat – 4/9/52: IFC Vol. 1312:139.
3. A sheaf of straw to find a drowned person's body – 13/9/51: IFC Vol. 1224:210.
4. Bartholomew's Day – 18/9/51: IFC Vol. 1224:261. Other versions of this particular legend about Bartholomew's Day were collected by Tadhg Ó Murchú from Diarmaid Ó Sé, Fán Shliabh [13/9/51], IFC Vol 1224:33–35 and also from Donncha Ó Rócháin, Droinn na mBéilleac [10/5/39], IFC Vol 623:327–29. Riobárd P Breathnach suggests that the terror connected with the name of Bartholomew arises from an ancient memory associated with the old tradition of this personality (C. Ó Síocháin, *The Man From Cape Clear – The Life of an Islandman*, translated by Riobárd P. Breatnach (Cork: Mercier Press, 1975), p. 150–51). Daithí Ó hÓgáin says that the name Partolán (Bartholomew) is an Irish adaptation of Bartholomaeus which Saint Jerome said meant 'son of him who stays the waters'. Ó hÓgáin also says that the tradition attached to Partolán was an 'invention of the early medieval historians' (D. Ó hÓgáin, *Myth, Legend and Romance – An Encyclopaedia Of Irish Folk Tradition* (London, Ryan Publishing Co. Ltd, 1990), p. 355). Quite a number of other fishing beliefs were collected by Tadhg Ó Murchú from Pádraig Ó Laochdha, Kilcatherine, IFC Vol 1224:348–50, 354–56, and Diarmaid Ó Sé, Fán Shliabh, IFC Vol 1224:93–4, during the month of September 1951.
5. The mermaid and *Paddy na mBó* [Paddy of the Cows] – 13/9/51: IFC Vol 1224: 210–13. Diarmaid Ó Sé, Fán Shliabh also told [8/9/51] of a contact between *Paddy na mBó* and two women from the sea, which resulted in great success at fishing, IFC Vol. 1224:4–6. Other incidents concerning contacts between humans and mermaids were described by Donncha Ó Rócháin, Doirín na mBéilleac [10/5/39], IFC Vol. 623:312–13, and Diarmaid Ó Sé, Fán Shliabh [24/7/50], IFC Vol. 1188:240–44. The legend of the mermaid's cloak being stolen by a man and her subsequent life with him is listed as one of the Migratory Legends [No. 4080] by Christiansen under the title 'The Seal Woman', R. Th. Christiansen, *The Migratory Legends* (FF Communications 175, Helsinki 1958), p. 75. This legend has been collected frequently in Ireland and was very common in the Gaeltacht areas. The theme has been used by poets in both Irish and English and this point has been thoroughly discussed by Bo Almqvist in his article 'Of Mermaids and Marriages', *Béaloideas* 58 (1990), p. 1–74. Patricia Lysaght includes a map showing the places in which the legend has been collected in her book *The Banshee – The Irish Supernatural Death-Messenger* (Dublin, The Glendale Press, 1986), p. 161. Descriptions of incidents involving encounters with fairy boats *[báid sí]* were collected from Micheál Ó Dúnaí, Kilcatherine [16/5/39], IFC Vol. 623:559–62; Donncha Ó Rócháin, Kilcatherine [10/5/39], IFC Vol. 623:309–12; and Diarmaid Ó Sé, Fán Shliabh [8/9/51], IFC Vol. 1224:7–8, [13/9/51], IFC Vol. 1224:35–8.

FARMING – FARM AND DOMESTIC ANIMALS

1. Calving – rubbing salt on the calf – 11/9/51: IFC Vol. 1224:200.
2. Putting a blessed candle under the cow – 11/9/51: IFC Vol. 1224:200. Concerning the powers of fire as it affects the newly-calved cow, I collected the following anecdote near Eyeries village. Does it provide evidence that the use of the blessed candle in this situation is connected with an ancient belief in the supernatural power of fire itself?

> Johnny Healy's father went to Kenmare with pigs. He was selling pigs, you know – there used to be a pig fair in Kenmare – so he asked Johnny – Johnny was only quite a young lad – so he asked Johnny to go out fishing instead of himself, you know, for that one night. So, they had no timepiece – no clock – but there was a bright moon there and the bright moon fooled Johnny and he went away down to the pier hours before the proper time. So, he was down on the pier all alone and he saw a light in this house about two hundred yards from the pier and he knew that there was an old man and an old woman living there – very old. They had two cows and it was very late, of course, in the night. And he moved up towards the house to see what was going on: there were no blinds, of course, in the windows at that time, or anything, you know. So he looked – it was in the cowhouse the light was – and he stole up as close as he could get to the door of the cowhouse but he still kept under cover. And he watched what was … he looked in and he saw there was a cow just after calving. And the old man and the old woman were inside, one on each side of the cow. And they had fire in a saucepan and one of them used to hand the saucepan of fire across under the cow's belly and hand it back to the other one over her back and so on until they did it several times, you know? And Johnny went back down to the pier afterwards and when the rest of the men came along going fishing, Jack Sheehan the stonemason was listening. Johnny started to tell the yarn, you know, and Jack Sheehan listened to him. So Jack says when Johnny was finished: 'Johnny,' says he, 'you didn't think,' he says, 'when you left the house last night that you would be the godfather of a calf before morning!'

Recorded on tape by Martin Verling from John Harrington (Caupey), Boffickel (who was born in Rinn Troisc, Allihies Parish and reared in Ballycrovane), Easter 1984.
3. The biestings being placed over the fire – 11/9/51: IFC Vol. 1224:200.
4. The cows' hooves – 11/9/51: IFC Vol. 1224:205.
5. Driving stock to the mountain – 21/9/51: IFC Vol. 1224:268. The practice of transhumance (transferring stock to summer pasture) was common in Ireland in the past and survived into the 1930s and 1940s on Achill Island, Co. Mayo (P. Ó Moghráin, 'Some Mayo Traditions of the Buaile', *Béaloideas* 13 (1943), p. 161–72). The Irish word *buaile* refers to the milking-place in summer pasturage or transhumance site and is often referred to by its Hiberno-English equivalent 'booley'. For further information on transhumance in Ireland see Jean M. Graham, 'Transhumance in Ireland', *Advancement of Science*, 10 (1953), pp. 74–79 and C. Ó Danachair, 'Traces of the Buaile in the Galtee Mountains', *JRSAI* 75 (1945), p. 248–52. For discussions on transhumance in Europe in general, see E. E. Evans 'Transhumance in Europe', *Geography*, 25 (1940), p. 172–80.
6. The goodness of the light brown cow – 18/9/51: IFC Vol. 1224:252.
7. The first stripping – 24/9/51: IFC Vol. 1224:294–95.
8. A prohibition against allowing milk out of the house – 11/9/51: IFC Vol. 1224:201.
9. Making the Sign of the Cross over the cow – 11/9/51: IFC Vol. 1224:201.
10. Smearing with dung – 11/9/51: IFC Vol. 1224:201.

11. The cow that went dry and died – 11/9/51: IFC Vol. 1224:190–91.
12. A hare milking a cow – 11/9/51: IFC Vol. 1224:189–90. Pádraig Ó Murchú (Patsy Gort Broc) of Gort Broc, Kilcatherine provided a story about a man from Kilgarvan, Co. Kerry who bought a cow from a man from Glenbeg near Ardgroom, Co. Cork. The cow was followed all the way to Kilgarvan by a hare which had already been milking it and the Kilgarvan man had to sell the cow himself (M. Verling, *Gort Broc*, p. 169–71).
13. The foal – 18/9/51: IFC Vol. 1224:252.
14. The donkey man – 24/9/51: IFC Vol. 1224:306.
15. The speech of the animals – 24/9/51: IFC Vol. 1224:306.
16. A prohibition against moving a cat from the old house – 21/9/51: IFC Vol. 1224: 272.
17. A prohibition against putting the dog after animals at night-time – 19/9/51: IFC Vol. 1224:255–56.
18. 'Hens a plenty and few cocks' – 25/7/50: IFC Vol. 1188:277–79.
19. The egg of the black chicken – 13/9/51: IFC Vol. 1224:221.
20. 'As dear as the two eggs for a penny' – 13/9/51: IFC Vol. 1224:219–20.
21. The March cock – 13/9/51: IFC Vol. 1224:220–21 Tadhg Ó Murchú collected a short tale involving the powers of the March cock from Pádraig Ó Murchú (Patsy Gort Broc). See Verling, *Gort Broc*, p. 167–69.
22. The cock's crow – 13/9/51: IFC Vol. 1224:221–22.

Farming – Tillage, Digging and Spades
1. The setting of the potatoes – 19/9/51: IFC Vol. 1224:261.
2. The blackening of the potatoes – 21/9/51: IFC Vol. 1224:266.
3. The Christmas ridge (i) – 21/9/51: IFC Vol. 1224:266.
4. The Christmas ridge (ii) – 25/7/50: IFC Vol. 1188:270–71.
5. Beliefs concerning the spade (i) – 24/9/51: IFC Vol. 1224:298.
6. Beliefs concerning the spade (ii) – 18/9/51: IFC Vol. 1224:247–48.
7. Flax – 21/9/51: IFC Vol. 1224:279–80.

Beliefs About the Houses of the People
1. The closed door – 21/9/51: IFC Vol. 1224:273.
2. A glowing sod being carried around a new house – 21/9/51: IFC Vol. 1224:272.
3. Moving house on a Saturday – 21/9/51: IFC Vol. 1224:272.
4. Sleeping in the new house – 21/9/51: IFC Vol. 1224:272–73.
5. Coins under the corners of the house – 21/9/51: IFC Vol. 1224:270–72.
6. A house on an old path – 15/9/51: IFC Vol. 1224:232–34.
7. Building onto a house – 15/9/51: IFC Vol. 1224:233–34.
8. A linny on an old road – 15/9/51: IFC Vol. 1224:234–35. The word *linny* is still frequently used in Eyeries Parish for a lean-to. The word was also used across Kenmare Bay in Uíbh Ráthach, Co. Kerry for an open shed beside a house, C. Nic Pháidín, *Cnuasach Focal Ó Uíbh Ráthach* (Baile Átha Cliath: Acadamh Ríoga na hÉireann, Deascán Foclóireachta 6, eag. gin. Tomás de Bhaldraithe, 1987), p. 72.

Trades
1. Cutting rods during the November moon – 24/9/51: IFC Vol. 1224:299.
2. The blacking hole – 24/9/51: IFC Vol. 1224:299–300.
3. Dyeing – 24/9/51: IFC Vol. 1224:298–99.
4. The making of candles in Kilcatherine – 25/7/50: IFC Vol. 1188:271–73.
5. The making of old oil lamps – 25/7/50: IFC Vol. 1188:273.

6. A little splinter hurdle – 25/7/50: IFC Vol. 1188:273.

7. Séamus of the ropes – 25/7/50: IFC Vol. 1188:273–77. The ropemaker in this case was almost certainly Séamus O'Sullivan who lived in a place called Lios na gCat to the east of Ardgroom village. Séamus' mother came from Carraig an Eidhinn in Co. Kerry. Séamus married Catherine O'Sullivan from Doire Mheigil. They had four daughters: 1) Joan (June 1871), went to New York; 2) Margaret (10 October 1873), married an O'Leary man from Co. Kerry; 3) Mary (10 September 1873); 4) Kate (18 January 1882), went to New York. Séamus had a sister called Sheila married to Denis Mullins (Mulliheen) who lived near the little bridge which is on the border between Lios na gCat and Ceapa Clochráin. It seems quite likely that this was the sister who was with him when he died. It was said that some of his ropes were on the roof of an old house which was about twenty yards east of the Holly Bar in Ardgroom village (O'Dwyer, *Who Were My Ancestors – Eyeries*, p. 16). For a detailed discussion of the various uses of bog wood in Ireland see A. T. Lucas, 'Bog Wood: A Study in Rural Economy', *Béaloideas*, 23 (1954), p 71–134.

The making of snuff – 3/9/52: IFC Vol. 1312:135–36. Regarding tobacco, that other great luxury of the people of rural Ireland, Tadhg Ó Murchú collected a story in verse in praise of it from Pádraig Ó Laochdha, Kilcatherine [3/5/92] which leaves us in no doubt as to the high regard in which it was held: An old couple from near Lauragh, Co. Kerry who were walking the roads called at the informant's house. They were both smoking. They asked the informant if he ever heard the poem, 'In praise of tobacco'. The old woman recited it for him (IFC Vol. 1312: 131):

> This is the tobacco that came from the Island on
> the third day of summer,
> That was saved and dried,
> That was turned and well turned,
> That was turned and not too turned:
> It had the taste of honey and the smell of
> sweet apples:
> It would take the sneeze from the nose,
> The fart from the behind,
> The decay from the tooth,
> And the devil from the soul together.

## The Community (pp. 38–46)

1. Schooldays in Kilcatherine – 21/9/51: IFC Vol. 1224:276–79. The schoolteacher Stephen McCarthy was nicknamed 'Master Mac'. He was born in Canfie and was married to Margaret O'Neill from Sliabh, Ardgroom. They lived in Ardgroom for a couple of years before he went teaching in Ballycrovane. Stephen was the principal teacher in Urhan after that and he then lived in Gort, Urhan. Stephen and Margaret had eight children (O'Dwyer, *Who Were My Ancestors – Eyeries*, p. 236). Tadhg Ó Murchú collected a reference to another schoolteacher from Pádraig Ó Laochdha, Kilcatherine [3/9/52] who was probably a hedge schoolmaster. This man's name was Daniel Houlihan and he lived in Kilcatherine Point. Apparently he used to write letters for his neighbours every Sunday after Mass, IFC Vol. 1312:127. See also M. Verling, *Gort Broc*, p. 248–51, where there is

a story 'An Fáth go bhFuil an Fharraige Suaite' ['The Reason Why the Sea is Restless'] which this old schoolmaster told to Micheál Ó Laochdha, a boat builder from Droinn a' Chríonaigh. The informant, Pádraig Ó Murchú, heard the story from Micheál Ó Laochdha.

2. An old school and schoolmaster in Ardgroom – 18/9/51: IFC Vol. 1224:242–43.

PUBLIC AFFAIRS
The post – 21/9/51: IFC Vol. 1224:268–69.

RELIGIOUS MATTERS, CHURCHES, GRAVEYARDS, PRIESTS AND STATIONS
1. Improper baptism – 11/9/51: IFC Vol. 1224:172–74.
2. Going for confirmation – 18/9/51: IFC Vol. 1224:246.
3. Kilcatherine church (i) the iron cat – 9/9/5: IFC Vol. 1224:152–53. An item concerning the removal of the baptismal font from Kilcatherine Church and its subsequent mysterious return was collected from Pádraig Ó Laochdha, Kilcatherine in 1950. The same item also mentions the so called 'iron cat' (Dept. of Irish Folklore, University College Dublin, tape M906c–M912a). The 'iron cat' is in fact a carved stone head over the entrance to the church on the southern side (Daniel M. O'Brien, *Beara – A Journey through History* (Castletownbere, Co. Cork: Beara Historical Society, 1991), p. 135), which, whatever its origin, certainly has nothing to do with the saint's name, *Caitiairn*, which has wrongly been interpreted as *cat iarainn* [iron cat].
4. Kilcatherine church (ii) a bull that died – 11/9/51: IFC Vol. 1224:163–66.
5. Kilcatherine church (iii) how a warship scattered the northern side of it – 9/9/51: IFC Vol. 1224:149–52.
6. Kilcatherine church (iv) the priest's grave – 9/9/51: IFC Vol. 1224:149. For further information about Kilcatherine church see Daniel M. O'Brien, *Beara – A Journey Through History*, p. 135–36.
7. *Clochán a' tSagairt* [the Priest's Cairn] (i) – 15/9/51: IFC Vol. 1224:230.
8. *Clochán a' tSagairt* [the Priest's Cairn] (ii) – priest hunting – 24/9/51: IFC Vol. 1224: 304–5.
9. Station bread (i) – 21/9/51: IFC Vol. 1224:269–70.
10. Station bread (ii) – 24/9/51: IFC Vol. 1224:307–9.

**Human Life (pp. 47–59)**

BIRTH
1. The birth mark – 9/9/51: IFC Vol. 1224:137–38.
2. A caul on a child's head – 11/9/51: IFC Vol. 1224:174–76.

THE WEDDING AND MARRIED LIFE
1. A married couple racing one another out of the church – 24/9/51: IFC Vol. 1224:311.
2. A prohibition against mothers – 24/9/51: IFC Vol. 1224:311.
3. The strawboys – 18/9/51: IFC Vol. 1224:263–64.
4. The stepfather who got rid of the child – 6/9/52: IFC Vol. 1312:140–42. For a comparison of child murders and dead child traditions in Irish and European Folklore see A. O'Connor, *Child Murdress and Dead Child Traditions* (Helsinki: Folk Fellows Communications No. 249, 1989).

SICKNESS
1. A bone that came out of a man – 15/9/51: IFC Vol. 1224:235.
2. A disease of the leg – 6/9/52: IFC Vol. 1312:146– 47.

DEATH

1. 'A respite until death' – 24/9/51: IFC Vol. 1224:296.
2. Provision for death – 24/9/51: IFC Vol. 1224:296–97.
3. The making of the coffin – 24/9/51: IFC Vol. 1224:292.
4. Opening the windows to leave out the soul – 24/9/51: IFC Vol. 1224:289–90.
5. Protecting the soul from the hounds – 24/9/51: IFC Vol. 1224:290.
6. The habit – 18/9/51: IFC Vol. 1224:246.
7. A prohibition against down – 24/9/51: IFC Vol. 1224:293.
8. Laying out the corpse – 24/9/51: IFC Vol. 1224:292.
9. The candles of the dead (i) – 24/9/51: IFC Vol. 1224:291–92.
10. The candles of the dead (ii) – 24/9/51: IFC Vol. 1224:292.
11. The wake pipes – 3/9/52: IFC Vol. 1312:136.
12. Keening the dead – 15/9/51: IFC Vol. 1224:222–23.
13. Leaving a person in charge of house and corpse – 24/9/51: IFC Vol. 1224:293.
14. Leaving things in the coffin – 24/9/51: IFC Vol. 1224:293–94.
15. A prohibition against crying – 24/9/51: IFC Vol. 1224:291.
16. Taking the corpse out of the house – 24/9/51: IFC Vol. 1224:292–63.
17. A prohibition against bringing a corpse into the house – 13/9/51: IFC Vol. 1224:210.
18. The Gap of the Dead and the Point of the Dead – 4/9/52: IFC Vol. 1312:139.
19. A prayer said going into the graveyard – 24/9/51: IFC Vol. 1224:288–89.
20. Women from Kilcatherine buried in Kerry – 4/9/52: IFC Vol. 1312:139.
21. The clothes of the dead – 9/9/51: IFC Vol. 1224:131–37. Seán Ó Súilleabháin has written a detailed description of this custom as it was practised in Tuosist Parish, Co. Kerry, just across the border from the informant's home. He also gives his opinions about the origins of the custom (S. Ó Súilleabháin, 'Two Death Customs in Ireland', *Studia Ethnographica Upsalensia* 9 (1956), p 211–15). It is also worth noting the memories of Noreen Heaney (the informant's granddaughter) of the custom ( Noreen Heaney (O'Sullivan) – Personal Correspondence, January, 1992). She also gave me an interesting account of the practice of the custom as seen by her brother. Following is this account, which I think indicates the seriousness of the belief – even up to recent times – in the need of the dead for clothes:

> People in our area at that time had very unusual customs with regards people's clothes when they died. Some adhered very rigidly to these customs, while others almost ignored them. One evening my brother Micheál called to S. house a few days after M. death. His daughter had all his clothes spread out on the bushes behind the house. She would take one garment at a time, run round the corner of the house and in a loud voice would call: 'M come back for your shirt', or whatever garment she had in her hand. Then she would run quickly back into the house, not daring to look over her shoulder lest she would see M. coming for his clothes. This went on, garment by garment, until all the clothes were back in the house. M. believed that by doing that her father would not want for clothes wherever he might be.

22. Sending things after a child – 24/9/51: IFC Vol. 1224:294.
23. The wedding suit being worn at a funeral – 24/9/51: IFC Vol. 1224:310–11.
24. The hair in eternity – 24/9/51: IFC Vol. 1224:29.
25. The bones of the dead – 24/9/51: IFC Vol. 1224:295–96.
26. Attracting the water – 24/9/51: IFC Vol. 1224:295.

DEALINGS BETWEEN LIVING AND DEAD

1. A woman whose sister came back to her – 15/9/51: IFC Vol. 1224:235–36.
2. The beetle heard at night – 24/9/51: IFC Vol. 1224:311–12. Tadhg Ó Murchú col-

lected from Micheál Ó Dúnaí, Kilcatherine [16/5/39] two accounts of encounters that the informant himself had with dead members of his own family, IFC Vol. 623:523–27, 527–33.

A very strong woman – 13/9/51: IFC Vol. 1224:217.

## Nature (pp. 60–61)

PLANTS
Woods in olden times – 18/9/51: IFC Vol. 1224:241–42.

MAMMALS
1. Tree cats and wild cats – 18/9/51: IFC Vol. 1224:255.
2. The fox – 3/9/52: IFC Vol. 1312: 135.

INSECTS
The devil's coach horse – 18/9/51: IFC Vol. 1224:243.

## Folk-Medicine (pp. 62–70)

CURES AND HERBS
1. Ivy for a burn – 24/9/51: IFC Vol. 1224:310.
2. Camomile (i) – 6/9/52: IFC Vol. 1312:143–44.
3. Camomile (ii) – 24/9/51: IFC Vol. 1224:286.
4. Cabbage – 24/9/51: IFC Vol. 1224:283.
5. *Liocán* – 24/9/51: IFC Vol. 1224:283– 84.
6. Plantain – 6/9/52: IFC Vol. 1312:145– 46. It seems likely that the plant referred to here is Ribwort Plantain *[Platago lanceolata]*. For further information on the folk-lore attached to this plant see N. Williams, *Díolam Luibheanna* (Baile Átha Cliath, Sáirséal agus Ó Marcaigh, 1993), p. 162–65.
7. *Cniubh* – 6/9/52: IFC Vol. 1312:147. It seems that the plant known more widely as *creamh* [Ramsons, *Allium ursinum*] was called *cneamh* in the parish of Dromad in Uíbh Ráthach, Co. Kerry (C. Nic Pháidín, *Cnuasach Focal ó Uíbh Ráthach*, p. 37). It is possible that this is the same plant as the *cniubh* mentioned by the informant here.
8. Comfrey – 24/9/51: IFC Vol. 1224:284–85.
9. *Luibh na hAbha* [the Herb of the River] – 6/9/52: IFC Vol. 1312:144–45.
10. Garlic – 13/9/51: IFC Vol. 1224:196.
11. Bad luck connected with herbs – 6/9/52: IFC Vol. 1312:144.
12. Wildfire (*ruacht*) – 24/9/51: IFC Vol. 1224:305.
13. Soil from the priest's tomb – 9/9/51: IFC Vol. 1224:138.
14. A cure in the soil from under hazel – 9/9/51: IFC Vol. 1224:138–39.
15. Leeching – 13/9/51: IFC Vol. 1224:197–200.
16. Bleeding animals – 13/9/51: IFC Vol. 1224:196–97.
17. The serpent's knot – a cure for blackleg – 13/9/51: IFC Vol. 1224:194–96. The woman mentioned here was Mary Lowney who was married to Seán O'Connell who had a shop in Lios na gCat (O'Dwyer, *Who Were My Ancestors – Eyeries*, p. 15). Mary was a daughter of Cornelius and Ellen Lowney from Bunskellig (O'Dwyer, *Who Were My Ancestors – Eyeries*, p. 35). Cornelius and Ellen had fourteen children. Mary died on 26 November 1905 at seventy-five years of age (O'Dwyer, *Who Were My Ancestors – Eyeries*, p. 15).

18. A cure for warts (i) – 24/9/51: IFC Vol. 1224:309.
19. A cure for warts (ii) – 24/9/51: IFC Vol. 1224:309–10.
20. A cure for headache – 9/9/51: IFC Vol. 1224:141–42.
21. An unusual cure for toothache – 24/9/51: IFC Vol. 1224:243–44.
22. Pulling teeth long ago – 18/9/51: IFC Vol. 1224:244–45.
23. The blood charm – 24/9/51: IFC Vol. 1224:285–86.
24. A green sod to stop bleeding – 24/9/51: IFC Vol. 1224:310.
25. Moss to stop bleeding – 24/9/51: IFC Vol. 1224:310.
26. Father Larkin and the bone woman – 24/9/51: IFC Vol. 1224:287–88.
27. A journey to Old Kenmare – a cure for an eye disease – 6/9/52: IFC Vol. 1312:
148–50. Donncha Ó Rócháin, Droinn na mBéilleac [10/5/39] described the use
of ferret's milk as a cure for whooping cough and also the use of a herb called
*Cuipíní an Triucha* for treatment of the same disease, IFC Vol. 623:321–22. Bríd Ní
Shíocháin from Inisfarnard Island witnessed the use of pieces of the vestments
of nine different priests as a cure for her brother's sore leg, IFC Vol. 1312:151–55
[6/9/52].

## Division of Time, Festivals and Pilgrimages (pp. 71–81)

TIMES OF THE YEAR OF SPECIAL IMPORTANCE
The Cross Day of the Year – 15/9/51: IFC Vol. 1224:228.

THE COMMON FESTIVALS
1. Shrove Night and the Skellig Lists – 18/9/51: IFC Vol. 1224:264–65.
2. Good Friday – 15/9/51: IFC Vol. 1224:228.
3. Patrick's cross – 13/9/51: IFC Vol. 1224:218.
4. Easter Sunday – 15/9/51: IFC Vol. 1224:228–29.
5. The signs of summer – 13/9/51: IFC Vol. 1224:204–5.
6. May Eve – 13/9/51: IFC Vol. 1224:209b.
7. Saint John's Eve – 13/9/51: IFC Vol. 1224:205–9b.
8. Hallowe'en – 15/9/51: IFC Vol. 1224:229–30.
9. The Christmas Block – 21/9/51: IFC Vol. 1224:267.
10. Christmas candles – 21/9/51: IFC Vol. 1224:267–68.
11. Saint Stephen's Day – 19/9/51: IFC Vol. 1224:265–66.
12. The Night of the Three Kings – 11/9/51: IFC Vol. 1224:182–83.

LOCAL FESTIVALS, PATTERNS AND PILGRIMAGES
1. The three tussocks in *Loch a' Coinleáin* – 9/9/51: IFC Vol. 1224:147–49. The ancient
pattern of Kilmakilloge takes place annually on 8 July and corresponds to the
feast of St Killian which falls on the same date in Wurzburg, Germany. This pattern which was formerly referred to as *Lá an Locha* [Lake Day] was of great religious and secular importance and attracted large numbers of people from all
over south Kerry and west Cork. For a very long time the religious pattern was
centered on *Loch a' Coinleáin* [Loch Mackeenlaun or Lough Quinlan] near Bunaw
in Tuosist parish, Co. Kerry. Another version of the legend of how the tussock
came to be lame was collected by Tadhg Ó Murchú from Donacha Ó Rócháin,
Droinn na mBéilleac [10/5/39], IFC Vol. 623:308–9. For examples of other oral
material concerning *Loch a' Coinleáin* and the pattern of Kilmakilloge, see M.
Verling, *Gort Broc*, p. 334–35 and for further details see also G. J. Lyne, 'The Pattern of Kilmakilloge,' *JKAHS*, 22 (1989).
2. Counting the rounds on the journey (i) – 11/9/51: IFC Vol. 1224:167.
3. Counting the rounds on the journey (ii) – 9/9/51: IFC Vol. 1224:139–40.

4. The Kenmare journey – 9/9/51: IFC Vol. 1224:140–41, 145.
5. Lady's Well – 9/9/51: IFC Vol. 1224:145–47.
6. Gobnait's Day – 18/9/51: IFC Vol. 1224:261–63.
7. The boundary journey – 9/9/51: IFC Vol. 142– 44.
8. *Cnoc na hUlla* – 24/9/51: IFC Vol. 1224:282. Cnoc na hUla is in the townland of Clogh-fune in the civil parish of Kilnamanagh (Allihies Parish). A pattern is held here on 29 June, the feast of St Michael (M. Mac Cárthaigh, 'Placenames of the Parish of Kilnamanagh (cont.),' *Dinnseanchas* VI, 2 (Nollaig, 1974):39).
9. *Ré Eidhneáin* – 24/9/51: IFC Vol. 1224:283.
10. *Ard na hUlla* – 24/9/51: IFC Vol. 1224:283.

### Popular Belief and Magic (pp. 82–91)

PEOPLE WITH SPECIAL POWERS
1. The midwife who had special knowledge – 11/9/51: IFC Vol. 1224:167–68.
2. Máire Ní Mhurchú and the hare – 9/9/51: IFC Vol. 1224:159–62. There is no doubt but that Máire Ní Mhurchú was a very important figure in the folklore of the people of Beara in the middle of the last century, as there are many references to her in the manuscripts of the Irish Folklore Department, mostly referring to that period. I have discussed her background (about which very little is known) as well as other matters relating to her elsewhere (Verling, *Leabhar Phádraig Uí Mhur-chú*, p. 538–42). Other items about her have been collected from Pádraig Ó Lao-chdha, Kilcatherine [1950], Dept. of Irish Folklore, University College Dublin, tape M906c–M912a and Donncha Ó Rócháin, Droinn na mBéilleac [10/5 /39], IFC Vol. 623:314–15, 316–18, 318–19.
3. Máire Ní Mhurchú and the girl who did her water in the pot – 18/9/51: IFC Vol. 1224:248–51.
4. Máire Ní Mhurchú and the woman who was abducted – 13/9/51: IFC Vol. 1224: 215–17. Tadhg Ó Murchú collected another version of this legend from Pádraig Ó Murchú (Patsy Gort Broc) on 28/4/39. It is interesting that Pádraig said it was a woman called O'Shea who was abducted and she was from Inward Ardgroom and it was into Puleen Strand that she was brought when she was freed. Indeed, in this version of the legend it was Máire Ní Mhurchú again who advised the woman's husband as to how she could be returned, Verling, *Gort Broc*, p. 157–59.

THE EVIL EYE
Bewitching – 13/9/51: IFC Vol. 1224:191–94.

THINGS WITH PROPERTIES OF MAGIC AND LUCK
1. The luck of the smoke – 13/9/51: IFC Vol. 1224:202–4.
2. The angel (i) – 13/9/51: IFC Vol. 1224:201–2. Pádraig Ó Murchú [Patsy Gort Broc] referred to the use of the Angel to protect butter (Verling, *Gort Broc*, p. 171–72).
3. The angel (ii) – 18/9/51: IFC Vol. 1224:245.
4. Spitting on money – 15/9/51: IFC Vol. 1224:227–28.
5. The four-leafed shamrock – 9/9/51: IFC Vol. 1224:155–57.
6. Stale urine – 18/9/51: IFC Vol. 1224:251.

POPULAR BELIEF – RIGHT AND WRONG
1. A prohibition against raking the ashes at night – 21/9/51: IFC Vol. 1224:274.
2. A prohibition against sleeping on the rack – 21/9/51: IFC Vol. 1224:275.
3. A prohibition against a lone person – 24/9/51: IFC Vol. 1224:312.

4. The feet water – 21/9/51: IFC Vol. 1224:274–75.
5. Having the clean water in at night – 21/9/51: IFC Vol. 1224:274. An item concerning a prohibition against skinning a dead cow was collected by Tadhg Ó Murchú from Diarmaid Ó Sé, Fán Shliabh [15/9/51], IFC Vol. 1224:61–63.

## The Mythological Tradition (pp. 92–107)

THE FAIRY HOST
1. A boy who heard the fairy music at night – 11/9/51: IFC Vol. 1224:168–71.
2. Fairy music, a match and activity on the mountain – 15/9/51: IFC Vol. 1224: 236–37. Another item concerning fairy music was collected by Tadhg Ó Murchú from Diarmaid Ó Sé, Fán Shliabh [8/9/51], IFC Vol. 1224:3–4.
3. Liam Dhonncha and the fairies – 15/9/51: IFC Vol. 1224:237–41. A man called William O'Sullivan was married to Mag (Jack) O'Sullivan in Canfie in the last century. Mag and William had six children. William was born in 1861 and he was a son of Donncha O'Sullivan and Kate Mullins from Canfie. This may very well have been the Liam Dhonncha mentioned here (O'Dwyer, *Who Were My Ancestors*, p. 17). As a further piece of evidence for this identification, William O'Sullivan died at nineteen years of age. It is clear from the manuscripts of the Dept. of Irish Folklore that this motif – [No. F331. *Mortal wins fairies gratitude by joining in their sport*] was reasonably common in Beara (S. Thompson, *Motif-Index of Folk Literature*, 6 vols. Bloomington Indiana 1955–58). Other stories concerning mortals taking part in the sport of fairies were collected from Micheál Ó Síocháin, Barra Coille 21/3/37: IFC Vol. 316:284–86 and Diarmaid Ó Sé, Fán Shliabh [15/9/51 and 17/9/51], IFC Vol. 1224:50–51, 76–79.
4. The midwife who was taken into the *lios* – 11/9/51: IFC Vol. 1224:176–78. See Reider Th. Christiansen, 'No. 5070, Midwife to the Fairies' in *The Migratory Legends – A Proposed List of Types with a Systematic Catalogue of Norwegian Variants* (Helsinki: Folk Fellows Communications 175, 1958), p. 91.
5. A cow that was carried off – 15/9/51: IFC Vol. 1224:63–5.
6. A sick man seen out riding – 9/9/51: IFC Vol. 1224:126–31.

POOKAS AND SPIRITS
1. A boy who was led astray on New Year's Eve – 18/9/51: IFC Vol. 1224:256–60.
2. A girl who was lifted into the air – 18/9/51: IFC Vol. 1224:252–55.
3. The Pooka of Darkness – 11/9/51: IFC Vol. 1224:181.
4. The Blackberry Pooka – 11/9/51: IFC Vol. 1224:181–82.
5. A light at night – 11/9/51: IFC Vol. 1224:171–72. Pádraig Ó Laochdha, Kilcatherine discussed with Tadhg Ó Murchú the prevalence of fear of the supernatural in former times. On the same occasion [1950] this informant related a number of incidents involving spirits (Dept. of Irish Folklore, University College Dublin., tape M906c–M912a). Quite a number of incidents involving encounters with various spirits and pookas were related to Tadhg Ó Murchú by Diarmaid Ó Sé, Fán Shliabh [17/9/51, IFC Vol. 1224:75–6; 20/9/51, IFC Vol. 1224:90–2, 96–8, 99–102; 25/9/51, IFC Vol. 1224:103–5, 106–9, 110–12, 112–14, 114–15, 118–20]. Micheál Ó Dúnaí, Kilcatherine talked to Tadhg Ó Murchú of an incident in which he protected himself from an evil spirit by means of the steel in his pocket knife [16/5/39], IFC Vol. 623:533–36. Donncha Ó Rócháin of Droinn na mBéilleac spoke to Tadhg about the different forms that the pooka takes [10/5/39], IFC Vol. 623:304–6 and also about a spirit that killed a horse [10/5/39], IFC Vol. 623:306–8.

1. The black hound and the priest – 9/9/51: IFC Vol. 1224:157–58. This story was also told to Tadhg Ó Murchú as a memorate by Diarmaid Ó Sé, Fán Shliabh [13/9/51], who said that he himself was one of the men who went to call the priest, IFC Vol. 1224:44–50.

2. The cows from the other world – 11/9/51: IFC Vol. 1224:185–89. Diarmaid Ó Sé, Fán Shliabh told other stories to Tadhg Ó Murchú of supernatural animals, e.g., a dog, [13/9/51], IFC Vol. 1224:43–44; a pig, [20/9/51], IFC Vol. 1224:88–9; a dog and a cow, [15/5/51], IFC Vol. 1224:52–61; a horse from the sea, [25/9/51], IFC Vol. 1224: 117–18; and one story in which he himself saw what he thought to be a horse but which disappeared when approached, [13/9/51], IFC Vol. 1224:40–3. The same informant also told a story of a man who had a frightening ride on a supernatural horse which had human speech, [25/9/51], IFC Vol. 1224:115–16. Micheál Ó Dúnaí, Kilcatherine also told stories to Tadhg of otherworld animals – a personal encounter with horses which cannot be seen, [16/5/39], IFC Vol. 623:536–46; a horse from the sea, [16/5/39], IFC Vol. 623:546–47; and cows from the sea, [16/5/39], IFC Vol. 623:547–48.

SUPERNATURAL PLACES

1. A closed door on a *lios* – 15/9/51: IFC Vol. 1224:230–31. *Comhla bhrea* (Speckled Door): door in rock, believed to provide an entrace to a fairy dwelling.

2. *Lios na gCat* [the *Lios* of the Cats] – 15/9/51: IFC Vol. 1224:231.

3. Máire Eoghain and the *Comhla Bhreac* [Speckled Door] of *Béal na Leapa* – 11/9/51: IFC Vol. 1224:183–85.

4. The old Eyeries road – 9/9/51: IFC Vol. 1224:158–59.

THE HAG OF BEARA

The Hag of Beara and the crab – 9/9/51: IFC Vol. 1224:153–55. Diarmaid Ó Sé, Fán Shliabh told of how a saint turned the Hag of Bere to stone, IFC Vol. 1224: 19–20 [10/5/51]. The boulder to which this tradition refers, known locally as *An Chailleach Bhéarrach*, is situated in the townland of Gort Garbh overlooking Bally-crovane Harbour. In another version of the legend of the origin of the boulder – collected by Pádraig Ó hAodha of Castletownbere from Síle Ní Laochdha of Eyeries, originally from Kilcatherine – Saint Gobnait is named as the saint who turns the Hag to stone, IFC Vol. 51:31–4 [1933]. Jim Harrington (Séamus a' Chápa), of Eyeries village (originally of Rinn Troisc), also told of an unfriendly encounter between the Hag and Saint Gobnait, IFC Vol. 51:45 [1933]. For more detailed information regarding the complex tradition of the Hag of Bere in Ireland and Scotland see Ó Cruadhlaoich (1988 and 1994–95), G. Ó Cruadhlaoich, 'Conti-nuity and Adaptation in Legends of Cailleach Bhéarra', *Béaloideas* 56 (1988), pp. 153–78. *Ibid*, 'Non-sovereignty Queen Aspects of the Otherworld Female in Irish Hag Legends: the Case of the Cailleach Bhéarra', *Béaloideas* 62–3 (1994–95), pp. 147– 62.

## Popular Oral Literature (pp. 108–113)

STORIES AND STORYTELLING

1. *Neil na gCopóg* [Nell of the Docks] – storyteller – 18/9/51: IFC Vol. 1224:245–46.

2. *Tadhg na Féithe* [Tadhg of Fay], Daniel O'Sullivan and other storytellers – 25/7/50: IFC Vol. 1188: 268–70. Tadhg na Féithe: There was a man called Tadhg (na Féithe) McCarthy living in Fay (An Fhéith), Gort Garbh (very near the place where the

informant was born) and he married a woman called Mary Houlihan in 1831. It is likely that this is the storyteller referred to by the informant here. Tadhg and Mary had three children and the last of them was born in 1853 (O'Dwyer, *Who Were My Ancestors – Eyeries*, p. 98), Daniel O'Sullivan. Daniel O'Sullivan (Breac) came from Doirín a' tSluaigh, in Bunaw, Tuosist Parish, Co. Kerry to Gurteen after the Famine. He had five sovereigns and five pounds when the Famine started and this helped him considerably to live through the worst of it. He was married to Nell O'Sullivan (Suaimhnis) from Colleros. Three of their children were born in Doirín a' tSluaigh and the fourth was born in Gurteen, *Ibid.*, p. 6. The informant had great respect for Daniel, who was still alive when she married into the farm in Gurteen in 1882 (memories of her grandmother written by Noreen Heaney [Noreen O'Sullivan], Glasnevin, Dublin, a daughter of Michael O'Sullivan, the informant's son – on the 28/12/92).

3. Ghost stories gone from the world now – 14/7/50: IFC Vol. 1188:258.

POETS

1. *Seán a' Bháin Mhóir* [Seán of Bán Mór] – poet – 24/9/51: IFC Vol. 1224:203–4. The poet referred to here is Seán Ó Súilleabháin (Seán Uaithne or Seán a' Bháin Mhóir) who was born in Glentrasna, Tuosist Parish, Co. Kerry around 1867. He married an O'Sullivan woman from Rosmackowen in Beara. Seán was buried in Castletownbere in 1910. The folklorist Seán Ó Súilleabháin collected some of his songs from his brother who lived in Doire a' Locha in Tuosist Parish (Ó Súilleabháin, *Diarmaid na Bolgaighe*, p. 133–40). Micheál Ó Síocháin of Barra Coille told Eoghan Ó Súilleabháin of how Seán a' Bháin Mhóir composed a little verse making fun of a servant girl in the big house at Dereen who would not allow him to light his pipe from the fire, [14/3/37], IFC Vol. 319:464–65.

2. A girl who had the gift of poetry – 24/9/51: IFC Vol. 1224:300–2.

3. Seán The Boy – 24/9/51: IFC Vol. 1224:302–3. It is said that the Downeys came to Scrathan in Urhan from Bunane, Co. Kerry – that three brothers came to Scrathan and three others went to America. One of the brothers who came to Scrathan was Seamus Bán Downey who married into a farm in Urhan when he wed Cáit Hurrig. The poet Seán 'The Boy' Downey, who is mentioned here, was the son of Seamus and Cáit. He married Margaret Murphy from a neighbouring farm and they had a son Seamus in 1844. (O'Dwyer, *Who Were My Ancestors – Eyeries*, p. 242). Tadhg Ó Murchú collected some other lore about Seán The Boy from Pádraig Ó Laochdha in Kilcatherine:

Seán the Boy was of the Downey family in Urhan. His son's son is there now and has a lodging house. It was he who composed the song 'An Mhaoil' ('*A Mhaol, a Mhaol do mhealais mé*'). He had some verses of it. The Boy was a lively lad. On another occasion he ran out of provisions, and he went to Castletown with a horse and cart for the provisions and he tied the horse to a stake at the side of the street. He went into the pub and I suppose he drank a drop over and above. But when he came out in the evening there wasn't a sign of the horse – some blackguard had released the horse while he was drinking in the pub. But he composed a song then, but I only have one verse of it:

| *Nách liomsa a bhí an mí ádh* | Wasn't I the lucky one |
| *An lá a thánag ón dtalamh aneas* | The day I came from the land to the south |
| *Ag díol chíos is Poor Law,* | Paying rent and Poor Law, |
| *Is gan criochán san ithir ag teacht,* | And not a *criochán* growing in the soil, |
| *Mo chapall sa tsráid go lá* | My horse in the street |

| 'Gus é ceangailthe ar staic, | Tied to a post, |
| Agus na linbh ag gárthaigh, | And the children bawling, |
| Is gan gráinne mine sa tsac. | And not a grain of meal in the sack. |

I only had the one verse. Oh, there was more in it no doubt (29/9/51: IFC.Vol. 1224:253–54).

A Song Composed by the Boy – Well, this is an old song I used to hear from my father long ago, that The Boy in Cathair (Cathair Caim I suppose) composed one about a trip he made to America. He composed the song after coming home, and I used to hear my father singing it, God rest his soul. The Boy was from Cathair Caim. He was a Downey, and that was the nickname he had. He was over in America and was terrified coming home by the gale and the bad weather, and he composed a song then after coming. This is how the song goes:

i

*Ó's ba ghnáth liom anonn is anall*
Oh and I was usually over and back
*Is níor liathadh riamh mo cheann,*
And my head never turned grey,
*Ach an lá do bhíos ar bhancaíbh na hÉireann,*
And the day I was on the banks of Ireland,
*Gur sciobadh uainn ár gcabhair,*
When our help was swept from us,
*An máta ba goire den cheann,*
The mate was nearest the bow,
*Is mé im sheasamh ar an mbowlsprit (bow-sprit) taobh leis.*
And I standing on the bowsprit beside him.
*Do chailleas féin mo mheabhair,*
I lost my senses,
*Is do bhíos i bhfad gan labhairt,*
And I was a long time without speaking,
*Nuair a chonac an shark ag damhas dár bh'féireacht,*
And I saw the shark dancing,
*Is mara bheadh Ard Rí an Domhain,*
And if it wasn't for the High King of the World,
*Do leag anuas ár namhaid,*
Who struck down our enemy,
*Ó ní thiocfaimís anall in aon chor.*
We would not have come over at all.

ii

*Ó's mo chreach agus mo léir,*
Oh my bitter sorrow,
*Mar an fhaid a mhairfead féin,*
Because as long as I live,
*Ní bhead i gceart im chéill ná im shláinte,*
I won't be right in my senses or in my health,
*Mar ó rugadh Mac Dé Oíche Nollag sa mhainséal,*
Because since the son of God was born on Christmas Night in the manger,
*Ní raibh a leithéid de ghaoth ná gála ann,*
There was never such a wind or gale,

*Do shéid ar nós an philéir,*
That blew like a bullet,
*Am na gcoileach do ghlaoch*
At the time of cock-crow
*Do chuir na céadta míle léig chun fáin sinn,*
And sent us hundreds of thousands of leagues astray,
*Is go mbainfimísne braon, mhuise,*
So that we would squeeze a drop,
*As chlochaibh glasa an tsléibhe,*
From the bare rocks of the mountain,
*Sinn ag screadaigh agus léic in ár n-árthach.*
And we screeching and a leak in our boat.

iii
*Ó's go dtabharfainn a bhfeaca riamh,*
And I would give all I ever saw,
*Ar an anam so a bhí im chliabh,*
And the soul in my breast,
*Bheith i's na Flaitheasaibh gan phian ná gabháltas,*
To be in Heaven without pain or possessions,
*Is go bhfuil mo shúilse anois le Dia,*
And now I hope to God,
*Ná beidh Sé liomsa dian,*
That He will not be hard on me,
*Mar nár dheineas aon droch-riail lem bháirthibh.*
Because I never did anything wrong in my life.

(13/5/39: IFC Vol. 623:399–402.)

SONGS AND SINGERS
1. Curley Creepy – an old singer – 8/9/51 & 15/9/51: IFC Vol. 1224:226–27.
2. A Song in Irish – *Cois na Leamhna* – 3/9/52: IFC Vol. 1312:137–38.
3. A fragment of a song from Iveragh – 3/9/52: IFC Vol. 1312:138–39.

BLESSINGS, WISHES AND A LITTLE VERSE
No. 1–8 – 11/9/51: IFC Vol. 1224:162–63.

## Popular Pastimes (pp. 114–115)

DANCING
25/7/50: IFC Vol. 1188:264–67.

## The Historical Tradition (pp. 116–117)

DANIEL O'CONNELL AND THE IRISH
15/9/51: IFC Vol. 1224:223–26.

# PERSONALITIES AND CHARACTERS

*These are not all 'people' in the strict sense of the word, but they all had a certain personality and character in the lore of Peig Minihane. I used English versions of names, surnames and associate surnames in the translation where I knew that these versions were currently used by the Beara people. In some cases, such as that of Máire Ní Mhurchú, the wisewoman, I have retained the Irish version where this is the version still used in current English conversation. I have placed the original Irish versions of names, as found in the manuscripts, in italics. Certain clarifications have been placed in square brackets.*

## PLACENAMES

*I used Irish versions of placenames in the English translation in any case where I was aware that this version was in current use in Beara, but in certain cases I have also given an English meaning in the translation. Where an English version has completely ousted the Irish one or become widely used I have used the English one in the translation. Regarding English versions, I have included both commonly used ones and explanatory ones in this index, as I do in the text. Where I have used English versions of placenames in this index I have given, in Italics, the Irish version as found in the original Irish manuscript, but with standardisation of spelling in some cases.*

SELECT BIBLIOGRAPHY

Aarne, A. & Thompson, S. *The Types of the Folktale*, 2 eds, Helsinki: Folk Fellows Communications 124, 1973.

Brennan Harvey, C. *Contemporary Irish Traditional Narrative – The English Language Tradition*, Berkeley, Los Angeles and London: University of California Press, 1992.

Butler, W. F. T. *Gleanings from Irish History*, London: Green and Co., 1925.

Christiansen, Reidar Th. *The Migratory Legends – A Proposed List of Types with a Systematic Catalogue of the Norwegian Variants*, Helsinki: Folk Fellows Communications 175, 1958.

Dègh, L. *Folktales and Society – Storytellers in a Hungarian Peasant Community*, Bloomington, Indiana: Indiana University Press, 1969.

Dundes, A. (ed.), *The Study of Folklore*, Englewood Cliffs, New Jersey: Prentice Hall, 1965.

Emmons, David M. *The Butte Irish – Class and Ethnicity in an American Mining Town 1875–1925*, Urbana and Chicago: University of Illinois Press, 1993.

Froude, J. A. *The Two Chiefs of Dunboy or An Irish Romance of the Last Century*, 2 eds, London: Longmans, Green and Co., 1891.

Henige, D. *Oral Historiography*, London: Longman, 1973.

Holbek, B. *Interpretation of Fairy Tales*, Helsinki: Folk Fellows Communications 239, 1987.

Jackson, K. *Scéalta ón mBlascaod*, Baile Átha Cliath: An Cumann le Béaloideas Éireann, 1968.

Jordan, R. A. and Kalcik, S. J. (ed.), *Women's Folklore, Women's Culture*, Philadelphia: University of Pennsylvania Press, 1985.

Larrington, C. *The Feminist Companion to Mythology*, London: Pandora, 1992.

Lysaght, P. *The Banshee – The Irish Supernatural Death-Messenger*, Dublin: The Glendale Press, 1986.

Nic Craith, M. *Malartú Teanga: An Ghaeilge i gCorcaigh sa Naoú hAois Déag*, Bremen: Cumann Eorpach Léann na hÉireann, 1993.

Nic Pháidín, C. *Cnuasach Focal ó Uíbh Ráthach*, Baile Átha Cliath: Acadamh Ríoga na hÉireann, 1987.

O'Brien, D. M. *Beara – A Journey Through History*, Castletownbere: Beara Historical Society, 1991.

Ó Cíobháin, B. *Toponomia Hiberniae 2: Placenames of Ireland – Paróiste Chill Chrócháin, Kilcrohane Parish (1)*, Dublin: An Foras Duibhneach, 1984.

O'Connor, A. *Child Murdress and Dead Child Traditions*, Helsinki: Folk Fellows Communications 249, 1989.

Ó Cróinín, S. & Ó Cróinín, D. *Scéalta Amhlaoibh Í Luínse*, Baile Átha Cliath: An Cumann le Béaloideas Éireann, 1971.

– *Seanchas Amhlaoibh Í Luínse*, Baile Átha Cliath: Comhairle Bhéaloideas Éireann, Scríbhinní Béaloidis – Folklore Studies 5, 1980.

– *Seanchas Ó Chairbre I*, Baile Átha Cliath: Comhairle Bhéaloideas Éireann, Scríbhinní Béaloidis – Folklore Studies 13, 1985.

Ó Danachair, C. *A Bibliography of Irish Ethnology and Folk Tradition*, Cork and Dublin: Mercier Press, 1978.

O'Dowd, A. *Spalpeens and Tattie Hokers – History and Folklore of the Irish Migratory Agricultural Worker in Ireland and Britain*, Dublin: Irish Academic Press, 1991.

Ó Duilearga, S. *Leabhar Sheáin Í Chonaill: Scéalta agus Seanchas ó Íbh Ráthach* (3 eag.), Baile Átha Cliath: Comhairle Bhéaloideas Éireann, Scríbhinní Béaloidis – Folklore Studies 3, 1977.

O'Dwyer, L. *Beara in Irish History*, New York: Vantage Press, 1977.

O'Dwyer, R. *Who Were My Ancestors – Genealogy (Family Trees) of the Eyeries Parish, Castletownbere, Co. Cork, Ireland*, Astoria 3 USA: Stevens Publishing Co., 1976.
— *Who Were My Ancestors – Genealogy (Family Trees) of the Allihies (Copper Mines) Parish, Castletownbere, Co. Cork, Ireland*, Astoria 3 USA: Stevens Publishing Co., 1988.
— *Who Were My Ancestors – Genealogy (Family Trees) of the Castletownbere Parish, Co. Cork, Ireland (Killaconenagh)*, Astoria 3 USA: Stevens Publishing Co., 1989.
Ó Gráda, C. *An Drochshaol – Béaloideas agus Amhráin*, Baile Átha Cliath: Coiscéim, 1994.
Ó hEochaidh, S., Ní Néill, M. & Ó Catháin, S. *Síscéalta ó Thír Chonaill*, Baile Átha Cliath: Comhairle Bhéaloideas Éireann, Scríbhinní Béaloidis – Folklore Studies 4, 1977.
Ó hÓgáin, D. *Myth, Legend and Romance – An Encyclopaedia Of Irish Folk Tradition*, London: Ryan Publishing Co. Ltd, 1990.
Ó Laoghaire, P. *Scéalaíocht na Mumhan*, Baile Átha Cliath: Pádraig Ó Briain, Clódóir, 1895.
Ó Síocháin, C. *The Man From Cape Clear – 'The Life of an Islandman'*, translated by Riobárd Breatnach, Cork and Dublin: Mercier Press, 1975.
Ó Súilleabháin, S. *Diarmaid na Bolgaighe agus a Chomharsain*, Baile Átha Cliath: Muintir Chathail, 1937.
– *Láimh-leabhar Béaloideasa*, Baile Átha Cliath: An Cumann le Béaloideas Éireann, 1937.
– *A Handbook of Irish Folklore*, Dublin: Folklore of Ireland Society, 1942; Hatsboro, Pennsylvania: Folklore Associates, 1963; Detroit: Singing Tree Press, 1970.
– *Caitheamh Aimsire Ar Thórraimh*, Baile Átha Cliath: An Clóchomhar Teoranta, 1961.
– *Irish Wake Amusements*, Cork and Dublin: Mercier Press, 1967.
Ó Súilleabháin, S. & Christiansen, Reider Th. *The Types of the Irish Folktale*, Helsinki: Folk Fellows Communications 188, 1963.
O'Sullivan, S. *Legends From Ireland*, London: B.T. Batsford Ltd, 1977.
Pentikäinen, J. *Oral Repertoire and World View – An Anthropological Study of Marina Takalo's Life History*, Helsinki: Folk Fellows Communications 219, 1987.
Póirtéir, C. *Glórtha Ón nGhorta – Béaloideas na Gaeilge agus an Gorta Mór*, Baile Átha Cliath: Coiscéim, 1996.
Ryan, M. *Biddy Early – Irish Wise Woman of Clare*, Cork and Dublin: Mercier Press, 1978.
Siikala, Anna-Leena. *Interpreting Oral Narrative*, Helsinki: Folk Fellows Communications 245, 1990.
Sullivan, T. D. *Bantry, Berehaven and the O'Sullivan Sept* (1 ed), 1908. Cork: Tower Books, 1978.
Thompson, S. *The Folktale*, Berkeley, Los Angeles and London: University of California Press, 1977.
– *Motif-Index of Folk-Literature*, 6 Iml. Bloomington, Indiana: University of Indiana Press, 1955–58.
Tower Hollis, S., Pershing, L. & Young, M. J. (eds), *Feminist Theory and the Study of Folklore*, Urbana and Chicago: University of Illinois Press, 1993.
Williams, N. *Díolam Luibheanna*, Baile Átha Cliath: Sáirséal agus Ó Marcaigh, 1993.
Williams, R. A. *The Berehaven Copper Mines, Allihies, Co. Cork, S.W. Ireland*, Sheffield: Northern Mine Research Society – British Mining No. 42, 1991.

## THE SEA'S REVENGE & other stories
Séamus Ó Grianna (Máire)
selected & edited by Nollaig Mac Congáil

Love, matchmaking, storytellers, emigration, feuding and fighting, Séamus Ó Grianna's subject matter revolves around the traditional life and lore of the Gaeltacht of his youth. His aim was never to be a modern, analytic, 'literary' writer but rather, like the seanchaí of old, to relate humorous, engaging stories and anecdotes in the rich, idiomatic Irish language.

## THE STONES & other stories
Daniel Corkery
selected & edited by Paul Delaney

Daniel Corkery's short stories rank amongst the finest in the history of Irish literature. His stories have been acclaimed and anthologised, and have exerted a profound influence on generations of Irish writers including Frank O'Connor, Seán O'Faoláin and Michael McLaverty. This new volume provides a comprehensive selection of these stories, and restores to print the work of one of Ireland's greatest storytellers.

## POETS & POETRY OF THE GREAT BLASKET
translated & edited by Séamus Ó Scannláin

Séamas Ó Scannláin has brought together the work of three poets: Piaras Feiritéar (1603–1653), Seán Ó Duínnlé (1812–1889), Mícheál Ó Gaoithín, whose lives were closely bound to the Blasket Island, spanning a period of over 350 years. This dual language anthology paints a picture of social change and linguistic evolution over those centuries.

## Another Time: Growing Up In Clare
Colette Dinan

Set in the forties and fifties, *Another Time* portrays the simple pastimes and day-to-day happenings in the small town of Scariff in Co. Clare. The town might have appeared sleepy on the outside, but a day never passed without some excitement. Colette Dinan brings to life the pleasant, friendly and resourceful lifestyle that existed in what seems another era.

## Méiní, The Blasket Nurse
Leslie Matson

*Méiní* is the lifestory of a remarkable woman, Méiní Dunleavy. Born in Massachusetts of Kerry parents, Méiní was reared in her grandparents' house in Dunquin. When she was nineteen, she eloped with an island widower to the Great Blasket, where she worked as a nurse and midwife for thirty-six years. Her story, reconstructed from her own accounts and those of friends and relatives, is an evocation of a forceful, spicy personality.

## Irish Country Households
Kevin Danaher

Most of the things which have become indispensable for us in our daily lives did not exist for our great-grandparents. The household work we now see as drudgery was accepted as completely normal in their time. Against the drudgery we can set the fact that there was less noise, less dirt, less pollution and less fear. In rural Ireland in the first half of this century, the way of life was simple, thrifty, holistic and in keeping with the rhythms of the natural world. *Irish Country Households* gives the reader a rare insight into the daily lives of those typical rural Irish families.